Challenge 2

Englisch für die Jahrgangsstufen 1 und 2

Workbook mit Mediensammlung

von
Jennifer Baer-Engel
Anne Herlyn
Annely Humphreys
Jason Humphreys
Joe Spencer
Dagmar Taylor

Ernst Klett Verlag GmbH
Stuttgart • Leipzig • Dortmund

Baden-Württemberg

Symbole

A1 🔈 Audioverweis

→ SB, p. 13 Verweis auf das Schulbuch Challenge, Jahrgangsstufen 1 und 2

Audios, Audioskripte und Lösungen zum Arbeitsheft online und in der App verfügbar!

1. Auf **schueler.klett.de** registrieren
2. Nutzer-Schlüssel oder QR Code einlösen
3. Digitale Medien online nutzen oder in die **Klett Lernen App** laden

Nutzer-Schlüssel
XAPG-APMU-FCpu

Ecological issues

1 Working with a cartoon

Use the words and phrases below to complete the sentences describing and analysing the cartoon.

on the man's chest | "Earth's resources" | robbing | standing next to a flower | represents mankind | pick off one of the petals | remaining | attitude towards Earth | ironic | an old tradition | handle | depleting | the planet Earth | "I love her ... I love her not ... I love her ..." | the truth

The cartoon shows a man ______________________ 1 whose head is the planet Earth. The word "mankind" is written ______________________ 2. The head of the flower, i.e. ______________________ 3, has two petals left. Each petal has a word written on it: together they say ______________________ 4. The man is about to ______________________ 5 and is saying ______________________ 6. The words in the speech bubble reflect ______________________ 7 whereby somebody who doesn't know if the person they love loves them back picks the petals off a flower, saying "She / He loves me, she / he loves me not ..." The words that are spoken for the last petal reflect ______________________ 8.

In the cartoon, the man, who ______________________ 9, is obviously unsure about his ______________________ 10. The cartoon deals with the question of whether we love the Earth, and how we ______________________ 11 its resources. It is ______________________ 12 that in the process of finding out if he really loves Earth, the man is taking away the last of its ______________________ 13 resources. The message of the cartoon is that we are very late in deciding if we really love the Earth and that we are still ______________________ 14 its resources. The cartoonist might be encouraging us to finally make up our minds, to decide that we really do care about our planet and stop ______________________ 15 it of its resources.

A1 2 **Listening: Forward Thinking: Eco-cities** → SB, p.13

a Before you listen, match the following words with the correct definition.

1. silver lining
2. urban development
3. perspective
4. landfill
5. vertical farming
6. to raise awareness

A plants grown for food along upright walls instead of on the ground
B a place where rubbish is dumped
C to improve knowledge and recognition
D sth good that comes from a bad situation
E the process of planning and designing cities
F a viewpoint or attitude towards sth, often positive

b Listen to the podcast and check which of the following topics are mentioned in connection with which city. Some of the topics can be matched with more than one city.

San Francisco

Singapore

Copenhagen

1. the fashion industry ______
2. vertical gardening ______
3. vertical farming ______
4. avoiding waste ______
5. green roofs ______
6. urban farming ______
7. bicycle paths ______
8. organic restaurants ______

c Listen again and complete the following sentences.

1. Instead of always being told what not to do, people should ______
2. In 2009, the city of San Francisco made it the law that ______
3. In Singapore, 500 kg of fruit and vegetables ______
4. In Copenhagen, the number of cycling accidents is lowered ______
5. The Copenhagen Fashion Week is trying to raise awareness of ______

A How to feed the world

1 Working with a diagram

Use the words and phrases below to complete the text describing and analysing the diagram.

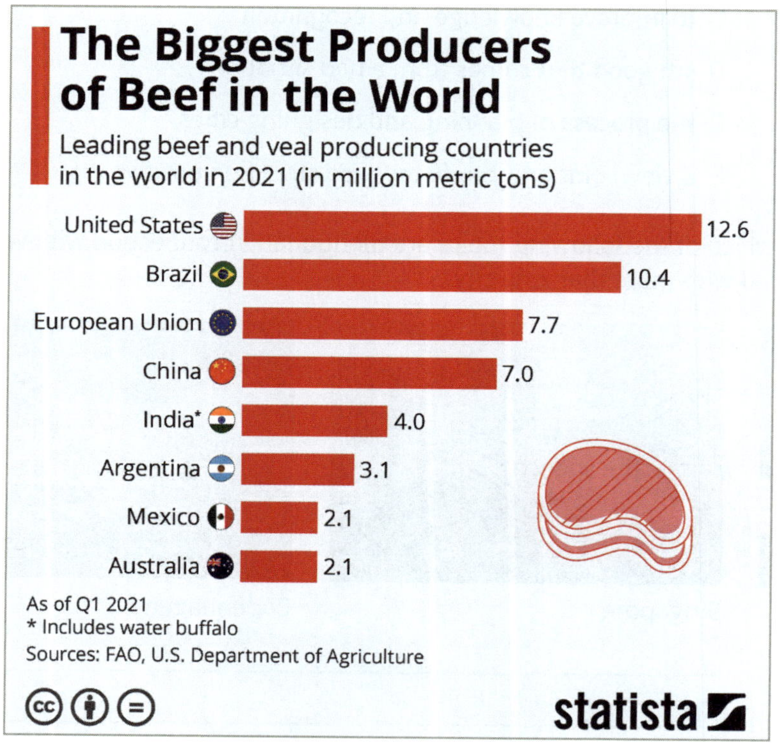

2.1 | 7.7 | 10.4 | 12.6 | Amazon rainforest | Argentina | at the top | bar chart | chopping | biggest producers | by far the most | China | followed by | global heating | grazing grounds | greatest polluters | high | India | lowest value | measured | meat industry | Midwest | populations | significantly contributes | water buffalo

The ________ 1 shows the ________ 2 of beef and veal in the world in the year 2021, ________ 3 in million metric tons. The country that produced ________ 4 beef in 2021 is the USA with ________ 5 million metric tons, ________ 6 Brazil with ________ 7 and the European Union with ________ 8. After the European Union comes ________ 9 with 7.0 million metric tons, then ________ 10 with 4.0 (including ________ 11) and ________ 12 with 3.1. The two countries with the ________ 13 in this diagram are Mexico and Australia, both with ________ 14 million metric tons. It is not surprising that the USA and Brazil are ________ 15 of this diagram, with the USA's vast ________ 16 for cattle, especially in the ________ 17, and its tradition of a sizeable ________ 18 since the 19th century, as well as Brazil's huge areas of pasture that have largely been gained through ________ 19 or burning down the ________ 20. Considering the sizes of their ________ 21, the production of beef in China and India is actually not that ________ 22. The beef industry ________ 23 to the production of greenhouse gases and thus to ________ 24. The USA and Brazil are therefore the two ________ 25 worldwide in this respect.

Writing a speech

→ SB, pp. 18–19

1 You are asked to prepare a speech on the topic "Conserving energy" in which you make suggestions on how we can protect the climate. Complete the introduction to the speech with your own ideas.

Dear audience,

I'm very excited to speak to you today about ______________________________

____

Have you ever thought about how much energy you use when you ______________________________

____

Let's look at some ideas of how we can ______________________________

____

2 Fill in the missing words in the main part of the speech.

And thirdly | but still | Did you know that | First of all | In any case | Secondly | So | think twice about | try to imagine | When you think of

__________ 1, let's simply use less energy. Cycle more, turn off your devices when you don't need them and use the internet less. Yes, you heard me right. __________ 2 one online search uses as much energy as a cup of tea? __________ 3, think about this before you watch your next video. The internet is great, __________ 4, we should only use it when necessary! __________ 5, think of the energy that goes into the production of the goods we use. Next time you plan to buy a new smartphone, __________ 6 whether it really needs to be a brand new one. Or can a refurbished second-hand one also do the job? And, it's not just the products themselves that matter. __________ 7 the packaging some things come in, __________ 8 how much energy went into producing that! __________ 9, avoiding packaging is good in more than one way – you produce less rubbish and conserve energy! __________ 10, while conserving energy remains the most important aspect, we also need to make sure that we get our energy from renewable sources.

3 Complete the conclusion to the speech using your own ideas.

We have seen that ______________________________

____

Please do not wait until ______________________________

We must start here and now to ______________________________

____

Thank you very much.

B Facing climate change

1 Listening: Forward Thinking: The UN's Sustainable Development Goals

a Before you listen to the podcast, look at the diagram and group the 17 goals into those which focus on environmental issues, those which concentrate more on social concerns and those which fit both categories.

SOCIAL CONCERNS

ENVIRONMENTAL ISSUES

BOTH

A2 b Listen to the podcast and answer the following questions using keywords.

1. What examples does Jerome give for the relationship between people's economic status and their attitude to environmental issues?

2. According to Abby, what is one of the causes of a large amount of poverty?

3. How does Abby explain the relationship between climate change and social problems?

4. What does Jerome say the word "clean" means with respect to water and energy?

5. Which functions of education are mentioned? Name two aspects.

6. To what extent does armed conflict prevent children from getting an education?

7. How are many women still at a disadvantage when it comes to work? Name two aspects.

8. According to Jerome, what can each of us do to help reach the UN's Sustainable Development Goals?

9. Why does Abby think that the idea of partnership for the goals is so important?

Talking about ability, permission, necessity → SB, p.24

1 Choose the correct modal auxiliaries to complete these sentences from a speech held at a demonstration in Canada against global heating.

1. We've demonstrated many times already, but we **might not / mustn't** stop.
2. In any case, we **must / can** continue to be loud in order to be heard!
3. We **may / need to** protest again and again.
4. Many people worldwide already **can / have to** leave their homes because of droughts or floods.
5. We **mustn't / needn't** look away.
6. Instead we **might / ought to** show solidarity with people in those regions that are most affected.
7. Even here in Canada, we **can / might** no longer deny the effects of global heating.
8. We **needn't / shouldn't** believe that buying an electric car or going vegan can solve the problem.
9. All countries worldwide **might / need to** get together and reduce carbon emissions significantly.
10. We **can / must** continue to demand change by hitting the streets again and again.

2 Look at the signs about what or what not to do to protect the environment. Write one positive and one negative sentence for each picture using these modal auxiliaries.

may not | must | must not | need to | ought to | should | should not | need to | ought to

Reuse and refurbish

Conserve water

Protect forests

Save electricity

Protect the oceans

Keep our streets clean

	Dos ☺	Don'ts ☹
A		
B		
C		
D		
E		
F		

C The blue planet

1 Words matter → SB, pp. 26–27

a Read the text and find at least five words or phrases that are used in combination with 'plastic'.

Currents sweep a lot of plastik → 30
The world produces about 300M tons of plasik
80 ← plastic pieses, plastic bags → 81
microplastics → 87

b Find further words and phrases used in combination with 'trash' and 'plastic' and write them in the table below. You may use a monolingual dictionary to help you.

Words / phrases in combination with 'trash'	Words / phrases in combination with 'plastic'
trash bin	plastic recycling
trash TV	plastic use
~~trash~~	plastic waste
plastic trash	plastic trash

c Write three sentences about the problem of plastic waste using at least two of the words from exercise a or b in each sentence.

› The world produces about 300 milion tons of plastic
› Our dayly plastic use is dangerous especially single use plastic for example plastic bags.
› In the ocean the plactic pieses get smaler and smaler it creates microplastic

We shoul reduce our dayly plastic use especially single use plastic.

2 Writing a comment → SB, pp. 26–28

Write a paragraph in which you express your opinion on Lecomte's initiative and refer to the picture of a dolphin surrounded by plastic trash. Use the following sentence beginnings.

Ben Lecomte ist doing the right thing, its very impressive

In doing so, he tried to ______

When I read about this, I thought of a picture which him swims in the ocean and everywhere is plastic

The picture makes me feel very sad, because dolphins are so beautifull and inteigent anamals

I think that we need to reduce our dayly plastic waste, and switch to

In my opinion, Ben Lecomte's initiative manages / does not manage to ______ because ______

D Water shortage

1 Reading for gist → SB, pp. 29–31

Put the following events in the story in chronological order.

- ☐ People in the street discuss the situation.
- ☐ Alyssa's family and their neighbours gather in the street.
- ☐ Alyssa's mother wants to fill the dog's water bowl with water, but nothing comes out of the kitchen faucet.
- ☐ Alyssa's brother Garrett gets a bottle of drink out of the fridge and starts to drink from it, and Alyssa tells him to stop and put it back.
- ☐ Alyssa takes stock of what drinks the family still has in the fridge.
- ☐ The TV broadcasts a press conference in which the governor announces that all water resources are temporarily rerouted to critical services.
- ☐ On the TV, it is reported that Arizona and Nevada have closed their floodgates on all the dams, meaning that the Colorado River won't flow to California.

2 Reading for detail → SB, pp. 29–31

Look at the passages that convey the thoughts and feelings of the characters. Complete the table with your results.

Passages conveying thoughts and feelings	Which feelings are conveyed?	Who has these feelings?

1 Lesen und Schreiben → SB, pp. 35–36

milos ...

1 Words matter

Match the words to form collocations used in the text. Then match each collocation with the correct definition.

1. competitively
2. cost
3. default
4. to face
5. mutually
6. pressing
7. supply
8. value

A a threat
B chain
C creation
D effective
E exclusive
F issue
G priced
H setting

1	2	3	4	5	6	7	8

1. to be confronted with a potentially dangerous situation ____________
2. the process of increasing the worth of goods ____________
3. the way a new device is automatically set up ____________
4. the process from production to sale of a product ____________
5. when two options cannot exist or be true at the same time ____________
6. not costing more than a similar product ____________
7. an urgent problem ____________
8. providing good value for the money that is spent on sth ____________

2 Focus on analysis

Find examples of the following stylistic devices in Prince Charles' speech and note down the effect they have on the audience.

Stylistic device	Example(s)	Effect(s) on the audience
1. enumeration (three examples)		
2. alliteration (one example)		
3. rhetorical question (two examples)		
4. direct address of the audience (three examples)		

2 Hörverstehen → SB, pp. 36–37

1 Before you listen, match each word with the correct definition.

1. biomass
2. extraordinary
3. niche
4. offshore
5. the backbone of sth
6. to offset sth
7. to reel

A in the ocean near the coast
B a plant- or animal-based energy source
C to stand unsteadily, e.g. if you are surprised or shocked
D only suitable in a small area or for a small target group
F to do sth to balance the effect of sth else
E the most important part of sth
G very unusual and surprising

A3 **2** Listen to the first part of the radio report and choose the correct statement.

In recent years, renewable energy in the UK has …

a ☐ been less reliable than fossil fuels.
b ☐ grown mainly in the forms of solar and hydro energy.
c ☐ become much cheaper to produce, especially offshore wind energy.

A4 **3** Listen to the second part of the radio report and choose the correct answer from the options (a, b or c) given below. There is only one correct answer.

1. The calculation of Britain's environmental goals does not include emissions caused by …
   a ☐ airplanes.
   b ☐ freight trains.
   c ☐ large tankers.
2. Closing down British steel plants will not help to solve the climate crisis because …
   a ☐ Britain does not produce much steel.
   b ☐ the country's steel industry is already being shut down.
   c ☐ steel produced in less environmentally friendly ways will be imported from other countries.
3. The price you pay for gas does not include …
   a ☐ any tax.
   b ☐ the cost of the raw materials.
   c ☐ the cost of the environmental problems it causes.
4. Steel from China is worse for the climate because …
   a ☐ more coal is used in its production.
   b ☐ imported coal is used to produce it.
   c ☐ it is transported around the country before it is exported.

3 Kommunikation → SB, p. 37

1 To help you prepare your monologue, collect aspects you could address by completing the word web.

Climate action

diagram

____

cartoon

dinosaurs, meteorite → extinction; ______

quotation

____

2 In your introduction, greet your audience and introduce the topic. Refer to your current situation and say why you are giving the presentation.

Hello, I'm honoured to speak to you today. My topic is particularly urgent ______

3 Develop your argument in the main part. Describe the problem using the message of the cartoon and suggest actions by referring to the diagram and the quotation.

We all know the story of how the dinosaurs became extinct. The cause was ______ 1. The consequence ______ 2. A cartoon I've recently seen draws a connection between the dinosaurs and ______ 3. In it, ______ 4.

It points out that ______ 5.

Now it's up to us to find out what ______ 6.

Look at this diagram – it shows ______ 7. We see that the largest amounts of energy ______ 8. Consequently, we must ______ 9. However, as David Attenborough points out, ______ 10.

4 In your conclusion, urge the audience to take up climate action.

And this is why I urge us all to turn this crisis around. We must ______

Science and technology

1 Working with cartoons → SB, pp. 38–39

a Look at the two cartoons relating to science and technology. Note down words and phrases connected to the cartoons.

"The good news is that higher crop yields mean that we'll be able to feed the world's increasing human population. The bad news is that as a result the population will increase even more, so we'll need even higher crop yields."

______________________________ ______________________________

______________________________ ______________________________

______________________________ ______________________________

______________________________ ______________________________

______________________________ ______________________________

______________________________ ______________________________

b Complete the following statements with your own ideas.

1. For me, the most interesting and promising area of science and technology is ______________ ______________ because ______________ ______________
2. If I had to name a famous person related to the field of science and technology, I would name ______________ ______________ because ______________ ______________
3. In my opinion, the most controversial scientific and technological inventions include ______________ ______________ because ______________ ______________
4. Arguably, the most useful scientific and technological inventions include ______________ ______________ because ______________ ______________

A A smarter world

1 Crossword puzzle: Data processing → SB, pp. 40–41

Complete the crossword puzzle with words from the text.

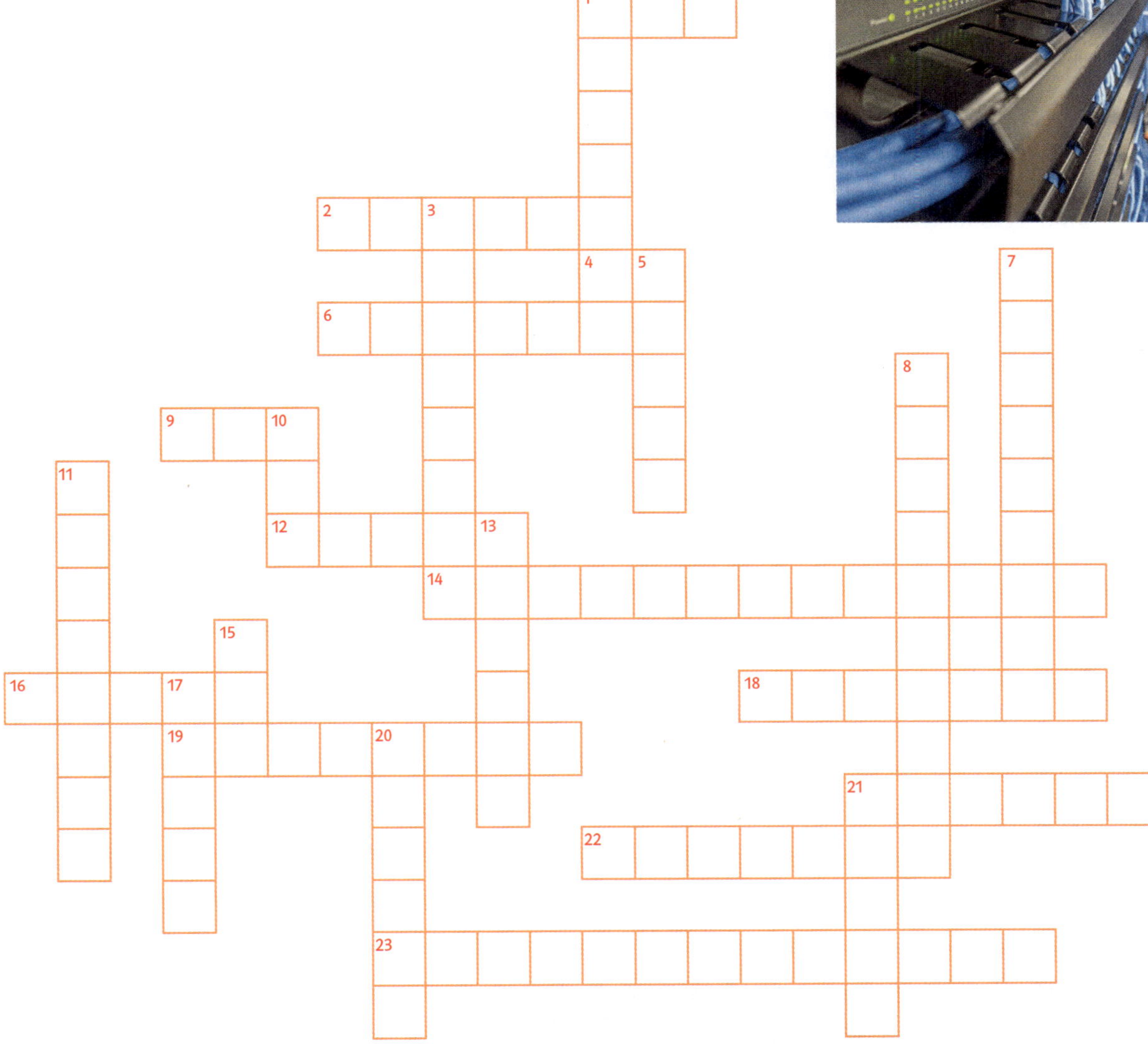

Across (→)

1. small computer programme, often used on mobile phones
2. to make certain
4. abbreviation of 'advertisement'
6. to examine sth in close detail
9. to record
12. controlled by computers
14. to distinguish
16. the car's license … contains numerous registration details
18. a regular, routine way in which sth is done
19. to record and store information
21. the author is woken up by his … phone
22. the first room the author enters in the morning
23. device registering the speed of an object

Down (↓)

1. the author's first name
3. famous American university the author works at
5. to deduct, e.g. from an account
7. device registering a change in air pressure
8. statement saying what might happen
10. a change of location is registered by a … receiver
11. the ability to move from one place to another
13. an official notice ordering you to pay a fine because you have done sth illegal while driving
15. amount of money that has to be paid
17. to follow the movements of sb/sth
20. a mobile phone … is picked up and the location of the device is stored
21. device measuring electricity and water consumption

2 Reading for detail → SB, pp. 40–41

Complete the table with the advantages and disadvantages of each aspect listed.

Aspect	Advantages	Disadvantages
1. Smart meters by utility companies (e.g. water, electricity) record many private details about how we live.		
2. Mobile phone companies keep a record of the location of our mobile phones using GPS. This data can be made available to other companies and organisations.		
3. Public traffic cameras can see from the number plates of our cars where we are at which time of the day.		
4. Many apps are linked to our bank accounts so that the banks know how we live and spend money.		
5. Insurance apps keep records of where and when we use our cars.		

B Benefits of innovative technologies

1 Reading for detail → SB, pp. 43–44

a Decide if the statements are true or false. Correct the false statements with a quote from the text.

Statement	True	False
1. Africa has strong infrastructure but a lack of skilled professionals.		
2. Other developing countries have already begun using digitalisation to make improvements in key areas.		
3. The most important thing is to educate and stimulate older people in employment, who can later pass their skills on to the younger generation.		

b Complete the summaries about the benefits of data in agriculture, healthcare, education and digital identification by using the words below.

scarcity | arrangements | improve | analysis | material | small-scale | reduce | diagnose | crime | financial | strengthen | teachers | profits | access

1. In Africa, 80 % of food production and almost 70 % of all work stems from ____________ farming. Data can enable farmers to ____________ their use of land and water, ____________ importation, improve food safety and make their own ____________.
2. AI can increase ____________ to healthcare in Africa for those groups who need it most. For example, it can ____________ illness and disease where there is a ____________ of medical professionals.
3. A national teacher platform provides ____________ with better, stronger ____________ and enables the ____________ of patterns of study.
4. Digital identification systems enable greater ____________ inclusion and less ____________ and dishonesty. Digital identities let people make their own personal financial ____________ and hence ____________ the economy.

2 Words matter → SB, pp. 43–44

Examine how adverbs and adjectives are used in the text and complete the table. Use a dictionary or thesaurus to help you.

Adverb/adjective	Positive/negative connotation	Rephrase in your own words
1. to hurtle headlong (ll. 4–5)		
2. a bold new path (ll. 13–14)		
3. a massive opportunity (l. 28)		
4. a massive infrastructure deficit (ll. 36–37)		
5. the most vulnerable and needy communities (ll. 61–62)		
6. a quick win (l. 75)		
7. better loans, better skills, better salaries (ll. 88–89)		
8. a high-performing digital ecosystem (ll. 90–91)		
9. a unique chance (l. 92)		
10. to move quickly (l. 97)		

A5 ## 3 Listening: Forward Thinking: Project Africa Digital

a Answer the following questions using keywords.

1. What is the aim of the project Africa Digital?

____

2. What does Jennifer say about young people's digital skills in MENA?

____

3. How do most Africans currently manage their money? Give examples.

____

b Complete the table with the key points on the following areas of digitalisation in Africa.

Internet access in Africa today	Internet and education
Internet and healthcare	**Examples of progress**

Talking about processes → SB, p. 47

1 Fact or fiction?

a Read the news tweets and try to guess whether they are fact or fiction by underlining them in green or red. Then change the sentences into the passive.

1. Doctors in China transplanted a part of a pig's eye into a human.

   ____

   ____

   🗨 105 ⇄ 82 ♥ 182

2. An English football team uses a robot coach to prepare team tactics.

   ____

   ____

   🗨 302 ⇄ 32 ♥ 74

3. Elon Musk and his girlfriend will build a house on Mars.

   ____

   ____

   🗨 202 ⇄ 96 ♥ 1532

4. Scientists in the USA have developed a vaccine that can cure all forms of cancer.

   ____

   ____

   🗨 752 ⇄ 352 ♥ 2146

5. Researchers have discovered a giant underground lake on Mars.

   ____

   ____

   🗨 32 ⇄ 15 ♥ 63

6. A team of Finnish scientists are producing food from electricity and air.

   ____

   ____

   🗨 36 ⇄ 21 ♥ 98

7. In Libya, a killer drone accidentally hunted down a human target.

   ____

   ____

   🗨 8 ⇄ 24 ♥ 151

b Go online to research whether the information given in the news tweets is true.

c Create your own factual and fictional news tweets on topics related to science and technology. Use the passive form and different tenses. Then let a partner guess what is fact and what is fiction.

____

____

____

____

____

____

Analysing the structure of a non-fictional text → SB, pp. 48–49

1 Match the types of non-fictional texts to their most likely overall structure.

Types of non-fictional texts	Overall structure
1. letter	A questions and answers
2. minutes	B editor's opinion on current events
3. editorial	C step-by-step description of processes
4. news article	D salutation, main part, complimentary close
5. self-help guide	E introduction, analysis of problems, strategies for dealing with problems
6. letter to the editor	F headline, lead paragraph, wh-questions, supporting details, background information
7. information leaflet	G addressee's details, salutation, main part (agreeing, contradicting or correcting), name of sender, town
8. construction manual	H place, date, time, list of people present and absent, record of decisions made and measures to be taken

1	2	3	4	5	6	7	8

2 Choose the correct answer to each of the following questions on text structure.

1. How can text structure be defined?
   - a ☐ The length of a text and how detailed it is.
   - b ☐ The length of the sentences in a piece of writing.
   - c ☐ The ordering of ideas, events and how this information is organised in a text.
2. What would you annotate or highlight when analysing the structure of a text?
   - a ☐ The amount and type of vocabulary used in the text.
   - b ☐ Whether or not the text includes a title to show what the text is about.
   - c ☐ Subheadings, paragraphs that differ in length and patterns (e.g. repetition).
3. What might be the most effective way for the author to evoke a reaction from the reader?
   - a ☐ Using paragraphs so the reader can process the information easily.
   - b ☐ Withholding information until later and using a short paragraph to emphasise an important point.
   - c ☐ Presenting the most important information at the beginning to quickly grab the reader's attention.
4. How are newspaper articles frequently structured?
   - a ☐ They have a lead paragraph, followed by details, ending with the least important facts.
   - b ☐ They start with background information, followed by a detailed and entertaining storyline.
   - c ☐ They start with the author's view, then go into detail with expert opinions, statistics and pictures.

C Genetic engineering

US journalist Dan Rather

1 Reading for detail → SB, pp. 51–52

Take notes on the information given in the text about Dan Rather (e.g. his life, experiences, thoughts).

2 Focus on analysis → SB, pp. 51–52

Study the excerpts and decide which structural features they contain: cause-and-effect relationship, comparison, contrast or repetition. Underline the words and phrases that helped you identify them.

Excerpt	Structural feature
1. "The idea of engineering human beings? Well, that was firmly the stuff of science fiction, like Aldous Huxley's dystopian novel *Brave New World* […]. It seemed as likely as, say, going to the moon." (ll. 14–20)	
2. "They tend not to be the type of people who hype things but when they talk about Crispr you can feel the urgency in their voices." (ll. 66–69)	
3. "If you are worried about your health or the health of your children. If you are concerned about how we might need to engineer our planet in the face of the climate crisis. If you are in finance, law or the world of tech." (ll. 71–76)	
4. "[…] I humbly submit that we as a species tend not to be good at thinking through where we are going until a crisis is already upon us. I fervently hope with Crispr that we can start the conversation sooner. That we can start it now. That's why we made the film." (ll. 80–86)	
5. "Crispr could cure genetic diseases such as sickle cell and Huntington's. It is being tested against cancers and HIV. It could also potentially be used to make crops more drought-resistant or food more nutritious. On the other hand, we are walking closer to a world Aldous Huxley foresaw." (ll. 97–104)	
6. "Science has given us the tools, but not the answers." (ll. 111–112)	
7. "We need to be informed. We need to be honest with what's real and what's not. And we need to add our voices to a global conversation." (ll. 112–115)	

3 Listening: Report about GMOs → SB, p. 53

a Before you listen, fill in the German translations for the following words from the listening text. Then add another word from the same word family. Use a bilingual dictionary to help you and compare your answer with a partner.

English	German	Words from the same word family
1. starvation		
2. fertilizer		
3. pesticide		
4. yield		
5. poverty		
6. nutrient		
7. to sustain		
8. variety		
9. deficiency		
10. harmful		
11. recipient		
12. implication		

A6 **b** Listen to the report about GMOs and decide whether the following statements are true or false.

	The report ...	True	False
1.	opens with a definition of genetic engineering.		
2.	does not go into detail regarding the problem of malnutrition.		
3.	mentions two different organisations.		
4.	gives nutritional details on genetically modified corn.		
5.	wants to inform about the opportunities and risks of GMO food.		
6.	clearly argues in favour of GM food.		

D Surveillance and state control

1 Words matter → SB, pp. 54–56

Choose the correct synonym for the following words taken from the text.

1. weariness (l. 13)	☐ frustration	☐ tiredness	☐ nervousness
2. increase (l. 16)	☐ rise	☐ change	☐ improvement
3. fury (l. 24)	☐ violence	☐ rage	☐ hatred
4. objective (l. 32)	☐ fair	☐ friendly	☐ neutral
5. to witness (l. 34)	☐ to discover	☐ to report	☐ to see
6. juvenile (l. 43)	☐ teenage	☐ imprudent	☐ dangerous
7. grievances (l. 53)	☐ wishes	☐ concerns	☐ demands
8. malevolent (l. 57)	☐ oppressive	☐ annoying	☐ sinister
9. curiosity (l. 68)	☐ accuracy	☐ inquisitiveness	☐ frequency

2 Reading for detail → SB, pp. 54–56

Write in the thought bubbles what George and Helen might be thinking about the other during the story.

George

Helen

1 Lesen und Schreiben → SB, pp. 61–62

1 Reading for gist

Explain what the following numbers from the text refer to. Use your own words.

1. 2018 (l. 33): ______
2. 460,000 (l. 53): ______
3. 700,000 (l. 56): ______
4. 149,403 (l. 57): ______
5. 360 (l. 105): ______

2 Reading for detail

To help you describe what Virtual Helsinki is and what it offers to its users, **paraphrase** (= express the same meaning with different words) the following sentences from the text.

1. "Virtual Helsinki – launched in late 2018 – is the physical capital's digital twin." (ll. 33–34)

   ______

2. "It was built using 3D modelling from open data […] as well as drawings and images." (ll. 34–37)

   ______

3. "It allows users to experience key landmarks as they choose, and it claims to be one of the world's most realistic VR experiences." (ll. 37–40)

   ______

4. "Helsinki is seeking to be a pioneer of sustainable tourism and allowing people to visit without racking up carbon emissions certainly aids that." (ll. 65–69)

   ______

3 Writing a comment

Complete the word web with ideas on how VR can have a positive effect on people's lives.

Positive effects of VR

- VR tourism
- VR parties and events
- VR museums and art galleries

4 Writing an email

Use the table below to collect your ideas regarding opportunities and risks of virtual tourism.

Opportunities	Risks

2 Hörverstehen

→ SB, pp. 62–63

A7–A9 **1** Match the words from the three listening texts with their correct definitions. Then listen and check your answers.

1. intersection	A an occurrence of death by accident, in war or from disease
2. offshoot	B to show too much respect or obedience
3. fatality	C not completely trusting sth
4. lidar	D the use of GPS or RFID technology to create a virtual geographic boundary
5. wary of sth	E the process of discussing sth with sb in order to reach an agreement
6. hostility	F a detection system based on the principle of radar but using laser beams
7. geofencing	G a point at which two or more things cross, especially a road junction
8. to kowtow	H to plan and direct the course of a vehicle, usually with the help of a map
9. to negotiate	I a company or an activity that has developed from an already existing one
10. to navigate	J unfriendly or aggressive behaviour towards sb/sth

Hörverstehen

1 Pre-listening

a Before you listen, think about why a country's government might collect data on its population, for example by conducting a census. Then complete the word web with your own ideas.

Purpose of a census

data collection
- *record information*
- ______
- ______
- ______

finances
- ______
- ______
- ______
- ______

services
- ______
- ______
- ______
- ______

b Take notes on arguments for and against conducting a census digitally in the table below.

Arguments for a digital census	Arguments against a digital census

2 Listening for gist

A10

Listen to the interview about a digital census planned in India. Choose the correct answer from the options (a, b or c) given below. There is only one correct answer.

1. How much of India's population has access to a smartphone?
   - a ☐ around half
   - b ☐ the majority
   - c ☐ less than half

2. Compared to men, how likely are women in India to have internet access?
   - a ☐ equally likely
   - b ☐ 50 % less likely
   - c ☐ five times more likely

3. What is the main problem with conducting a digital census in India?
   - a ☐ lack of high-speed internet in many regions
   - b ☐ the analysis of the data is going to be difficult
   - c ☐ large parts of the population are going to be excluded

A10 3 Listening for detail

a Listen again and answer the following questions in keywords.

1. Why might a household with a smartphone not be able to fill out the census? Name two reasons.

2. How did India rank in Dr Chakravorti's gender digital inclusion survey?

3. Which groups are most likely to be digitally excluded in India? Name two groups.

4. Why is it important that digitally excluded groups are given particular attention in a census?

b Complete the sentences about Dr Chakravorti's concerns.

1. The main problem with India's vaccination registration app was that

2. It is Dr Chakravorti's main concern that the Indian government

3. Dr Chakravorti predicts that

4 Post-listening

a How might a digital census turn out in your country? Use your knowledge about the pros and cons of a digital census and the following words and phrases to answer this question.

digital inclusion | data protection | paper-based | internet access | to feel comfortable doing sth | user-friendly | online portal | data storage | to have trouble doing sth | instructions

b Explain what, in your opinion, is the best way to increase digital inclusion.

Consumerism

A11 1 **Listening: Different ways of shopping**

a Listen to four young people talking about their shopping behaviours. Match the speakers (1–4) with the four pictures below.

b Listen again and take notes on how each speaker shops and why.

A

B

C

D

2 **Talking about consumer habits** → SB, p. 65

Describe your own consumer habits and explain what influences your shopping behaviour and choices.

A Shopping addiction

1 Reading for gist → SB, pp. 66–67

In your book, you are asked to **sum up** (= give a concise account of the main points) Dev's problem and **explain** (= describe and define in detail) how it affected his life. Go back to the text and answer the following questions.

1. What does Dev confess to the readers?

2. What has been problematic for Dev and what negative consequences did his previous behaviour have?

2 Reading for detail → SB, pp. 66–67

a In your book, you are asked to **explain** (= describe and define in detail) why shopping addiction is generally seen as a female issue. Answer the following questions.

1. What is seen as a "woman's territory" (l. 26)?

2. What is stereotypically regarded as a "woman's behaviour" (ll. 28–29)?

3. Why don't we hear about many men suffering from Dev's problem?

b You are asked to **describe** (= give a detailed account of) what happened when Dev started to look at things online. Answer the following questions.

1. What feelings does Dev often get when he browses through the internet at home after work?

2. What does he do when he gets these feelings?

3. What immediate influence do his online activities have on his state of mind?

c Now you are asked to **outline** (= give the main features of) how Dev came to realise that he had a problem and to what extent he is now 'cured'. Answer the following questions.

1. Why did Dev talk to a friend and how did she react?

2. What did Dev do after the conversation with his friend?

3. How does Dev deal with his addiction nowadays and what does he miss?

B Sustainable consumption

1 Reading for detail → SB, pp. 70–72

Read the text and complete the following sentences. Use your own words as far as possible.

1. There is confusion regarding the language of sustainability because ______________________________
2. Ethical production means that ______________________________
3. Cruelty-free products promise the consumer that ______________________________

4. Organic cotton is criticised for ______________________________
5. Principles of fair trade are, for example ______________________________
6. Instead of relying on a company's certification, it is sometimes more advisable to ______________________________
7. A product is only truly sustainable if ______________________________
8. A good example of greenwashing is ______________________________
9. In contrast to fast fashion, slow fashion means ______________________________

2 Words matter → SB, pp. 70–72

The following words are taken from the text. Find words that belong to the same word family and complete the table. You can use a bilingual or monolingual dictionary to help you.

Verb	Noun	Adjective	Adverb
	curiosity		
to produce			
	criticism		
to subscribe			
		exaggerated	
		additional	

3 Writing an email → SB, p.72

a Look at the email, which is a young reader's response to Aja's article. Fill in the gaps using the words below. There are three words you do not need.

labels | expensive | unsustainable | confusing | research | source | slow fashion | expensive | transparent | improvements | fast fashion | durable | convenient | enlightening | influencers

From:	...
To:	...
Subject:	Response to your article in *The Guardian*

Dear Aja,

I recently read your article "A guide to the language of sustainable fashion" published in *The Guardian* and found it quite ____________ 1.

I've always been interested in fashion, and more recently the environment.

You are absolutely right about all these different ____________ 2 – they can be very ____________ 3 for a consumer who wants to shop in a sustainable way. It's always best to do your own ____________ 4. Luckily, I've found brands which have ____________ 5 production processes. They offer information about how they ____________ 6 the raw materials for their products. Although they are ____________ 7, the clothes are extremely durable.

Some companies also offers a free-of-charge repair service.

Like you, I don't want to be a member of this ____________ 8 movement, that's why I have decided to buy high-quality and sustainable clothes rather than buying new stuff every month.

In my opinion, more people need to think this way and stop following trends. I hope the ____________ 9 out there help spread the word of ____________ 10 instead of promoting ____________ 11 clothes that cramp people's wardrobe.

I'd like to say thank you for talking about this important topic and I sincerely hope there will be big ____________ 12 in this area.

Best regards,

Finley

b Write down three questions you would like to ask Finley about what he says in his email.

____

____

____

____

____

C Working in advertising

1 Talking about marketing and advertising → SB, pp. 73–74

Read what Kay and Ben say about their work at Schmidt Travino Drew & Partners. Fill in the gaps with the words below.

interest | competitor | social media | ambush marketing | commercials | followers | services | gamification | promote | desire | audience | platforms | marketing strategy | purpose-driven marketing | influencers | target audience | announced | attention | apps

Kay, 23

When I was a kid, I used to like watching the ________ 1 on TV more than the shows themselves! I was fascinated by the way companies could use different methods to ________ 2 their products and ________ 3. Of course, you don't get that as much now as most TV is streamed, but the idea is still the same. You have to find the right way to talk to your ________ 4, grab their ________ 5 and create an ________ 6 in what you're selling, and a ________ 7 to buy it. Where I work, we don't really do much TV work anymore, but even when we work with social media ________ 8 or smartphone ________ 9, we still try and stick to the basic principles of marketing. And one area that we are increasingly involved in is ________ 10, where a good cause or narrative is often attached to the product or service on offer.

Ben, 26

I really enjoy it when a new project comes in. The first thing we do is think about which ________ 1 makes the most sense. If we are marketing something aimed at a younger ________ 2, then we need to place our ads where they're going to be seen – the smartphone. I have been involved in a lot of ________ 3 projects recently, where we have created simple games and challenges to keep customers coming back.

Of course, nowadays, companies have to have a presence on ________ 4, and the amount of ________ 5, popular or famous people with a large amount of ________ 6, has opened up a whole new industry. I still like a laugh, though. Probably my favourite project was from a major car company, which ________ 7 the release of its new model by congratulating its main ________ 8 on its 100th birthday. Now that is classic ________ 9 !

2 Listening: Forward Thinking: Marketing your business → SB, p.75

A12 **a** Listen to the first part of the podcast and choose the correct answer(s) from the options (a, b or c) given below. Sometimes more than one option can be correct.

1. Matilda lectures at the London School of Economics and also …
   - a ☐ writes books.
   - b ☐ works at a consulting company.
   - c ☐ runs her own consulting company.

2. Working with companies and start-ups makes up at least …
   - a ☐ 15% of her work.
   - b ☐ 40% of her work.
   - c ☐ 50% of her work.

3. Nowadays, advertising is competing with …
   - a ☐ social networks.
   - b ☐ streaming services.
   - c ☐ play stations and computer games.

A13 **b** Listen to the second part of the podcast. Select the best option to complete each statement.

1. The tonality of your marketing efforts should …
   - a ☐ convey authenticity.
   - b ☐ be formal and complex.
   - c ☐ alienate your target group.

2. Traditional methods of advertising are …
   - a ☐ vanishing.
   - b ☐ becoming too expensive.
   - c ☐ important and frequently used.

3. The purpose of guerrilla marketing is to …
   - a ☐ create attention.
   - b ☐ make people talk about the product.
   - c ☐ make the competitor's product look bad.

4. When designing an ad campaign, you should not forget the effectiveness of using …
   - a ☐ a powerful slogan.
   - b ☐ celebrities and stars.
   - c ☐ every marketing channel available.

Working with advertisements → SB, pp.76–77

1 Talking about and evaluating product packaging

floral | manly | angular | square | masculine | feminine | pump | lid | edges | spray | tassle | girly

a Choose a product and describe it.

____

____

b Say which product is the most attractive to you and why. What do you like about it?

____

____

c What do you think is the respective target market for each item? How does the packaging designer try to attract this particular target group? Take notes.

A ____

____

B ____

____

C ____

____

D ____

____

d Choose one of the products and think of a suitable name and slogan for it. Give reasons for your choice.

____

____

____

____

____

____

____

D Brands with purpose

1 Focus on grammar

Complete the text about REI and Anheuser-Busch with the verbs in brackets in the present perfect.

REI ____________ 1 (to see) over 200 retail companies go bankrupt since it launched its campaign. It believes it ____________ 2 (to remain) strong and profitable because it ____________ 3 (to keep) to its principles. Supporting its staff ____________ 4 (to allow) it to grow more associates. Additionally, it ____________ 5 (to always endorse) nonprofit partners. Anheuser-Busch ____________ 6 (to dedicate oneself) to water preservation for many years and ____________ 7 (to align) with other organisations to support conservation projects.

2 Working with a cartoon

a Describe the cartoon.

____
____
____
____
____
____
____
____
____
____
____
____
____

b Analyse the message of the cartoon.

____
____
____
____

c Relate the message of the cartoon to the text "The power of purpose". → SB, pp. 78–80

____
____
____
____

3 Focus on grammar

a Complete the text of an influencer describing his daily life with either the simple present or present progressive form of the verbs in brackets.

Hi, I'm Tom and I ______________ 1 (to work) as a fashion influencer, which means I ______________ 2 (to make) a living producing sponsored content for brands. I have 167,000 followers on Instagram and almost 20,000 YouTube subscribers. At the moment I ______________ 3 (to work) with around a dozen different fashion labels and I usually ______________ 4 (to create) one video or social media post a week for each. Normally my day ______________ 5 (to start) at about 10 am. I never ______________ 6 (to begin) earlier than 9 am! Many people think I have the dream job, but there is a lot of work involved. Every morning I ______________ 7 (to write) a plan for the day to ensure I make the most of my time. Being an influencer is definitely cool, but I know it isn't going to last forever. At the moment I ______________ 8 (to study) marketing at university and this is more of a hobby. I always ______________ 9 (to make sure) that I ______________ 10 (to go) to classes because I want to get good grades. Currently I ______________ 11 (to do) a lot of work for a big sportswear company and this morning I ______________ 12 (to shoot) a video for some new trainers. Usually I ______________ 13 (to work) from home but today I ______________ 14 (to go) to the local park as the company wants some outdoor shots. People often ______________ 15 (to ask) me what the best thing about being an influencer is. Of course, I ______________ 16 (to love) getting free stuff, but what I think I ______________ 17 (to enjoy) the most is being in contact with so many people.

b Tom is hosting a live webchat about being an influencer. Use the words below to form questions in the simple present or present progressive.

1. which – brands – you – currently – work with

   ____

2. you – any advice – about how to get started – have

   ____

3. payment – how – work

   ____

4. anything – you – about being an influencer – not like – that

   ____

5. which – you – at the moment – social media sites – use

   ____

1 Lesen und Schreiben

→ SB, pp. 84–85

1 Writing a blog post

To help you prepare your blog post, collect ideas by answering the following questions in note form.

1. How do you think you would feel if you moved into a tiny house?
   ____
2. What do you think you would miss the most?
   ____
3. What would you probably miss the least?
   ____
4. What would be the biggest challenge for you?
   ____
5. What would you like the most about living in a tiny house?
   ____
6. How do you think you would feel after 14 days?
   ____
7. How would you feel when the time is up? Would you be happy or sad to move out? Why?
   ____

2 Writing an argumentative essay

Use this table to collect pros and cons of living in a big mansion and living in a tiny house.

	Big mansion	Tiny house
Pros ☺		
Cons ☹		

2 Hörverstehen → SB, p. 86

A14 **1** Listen to the BBC podcast and answer the following questions in keywords.

1. How many pre-owned fashion items were sold on a big online platform last year?

___

2. According to Oxfam, how many items of clothing end up in landfills every week?

___

3. What did the climate change activism group "Extinction Rebellion" demand?

___

4. According to Caroline, what does "Fashion Week" want to promote?

___

5. Why, according to Simon, might seasonal collections be part of the issue of textile waste?

___

___

6. According to Caroline, what has to change in order to reduce the amount of clothes on landfills?

___

7. What is "Second-hand September"?

___

8. What did Oxfam do in 1974?

___

9. What, according to Fee, is responsible for the increasing amount of textile rubbish on landfills?

___

10. What effect has "Second-hand September" had on social media?

___

2 Before you listen to the report, match the words from the listening text with their definitions.

1. council tax
2. budgeting
3. tenancy
4. to flag up
5. mortgage

A the right to live in a building or use land in exchange for rent

B to warn or tell people that sth is important or is a problem

C money borrowed from a bank in order to buy a house or land

D an amount of money that people living in a particular area must pay annually for public services (e.g. waste collection)

E the process of calculating how much money you will have to earn or save during a particular period of time, and of planning how to spend it

A15 3 Listen to the report about a teenager and her money issues followed by the assessment of the Citizens' Advice Bureau. After listening, write a few sentences about your own experiences with debt and borrowing money from family, friends or a financial institution.

____

____

____

____

____

____

____

3 Kommunikation → SB, p. 87

1 To help you prepare your monologue, study the diagram in detail and fill in the missing words.

The ______________ 1 of the diagram is "Ad spending in the USA, 2018 & 2022, by media". We can see two ______________ 2. The chart on the ______________ 3 represents the spending on advertising in 2018, and the chart on the ______________ 4 shows the spending in 2022. Both charts are divided into seven ______________ 5. In 2018, most of the advertising budget, ______________ 6 percent, was spent on ______________ 7 advertising. By 2022, this had ______________ 8 significantly by ______________ 9 percent. Moreover, this type of advertising came to make up almost ______________ 10 of all spending on advertising.

At the same time, we can see that the spending on advertising for TV has ______________ 11 by ______________ 12 percent, from ______________ 13 percent to ______________ 14 percent. On the other hand, spending on advertising for ______________ 15 devices has more or less ______________ 16. It is interesting to see that spending on advertising for ______________ 17 has almost halved. Between 2018 and 2022, we can see a drop from ______________ 18 percent to ______________ 19 percent. It is also noteworthy that the share of print advertising is very ______________ 20. It can be assumed that this figure will ______________ 21 further in the future. The spending on advertising on radio only shows an insignificant decrease of ______________ 22 percent, from ______________ 23 percent to ______________ 24 percent. Out-of-home advertising and adverts in directories play a very ______________ 25 role as well. Both budgets experienced a ______________ 26 in 2022.

The diagram supports the overall impression that digital adverts are playing a more and more ______________ 27 role in the world of advertising. In the last decade there has been a very significant ______________ 28 from print to digital, which is also mirrored in this diagram.

Land of dreams?

A16 1 **Crossword puzzle: The USA – past and present** → SB, p. 89

Listen to the podcast "Forward Thinking: The USA – past and present" and fill in the crossword puzzle with words from the podcast.

Across (→)

2. There have been many accusations of … at the hands of the American police.
3. The goal of the Civil Rights Movement was to achieve … among all Americans.
5. Slavery was … in the USA in 1865.
8. The current space race, which is funded by private billionaires, can be seen as an example of the … spirit of the USA.
10. In the past, African people were forced to work on cotton, tobacco and sugar cane …
13. The American Dream makes people believe that the USA is a land of … opportunities.
14. On 6 January 2021 an angry mob stormed the … Building in Washington D.C.
15. The centre of information technology and innovation in the USA is located in … Valley in California.
16. The set of laws which determine how the US government works is called the …

Down (↓)

1. Barack Obama was the first US president with African …
4. Many important … were made in the USA, e.g. the telephone.
6. Virginia was one of the first British … on the North American continent.
7. Africans were brought to America as … people as early as the 17th century.
9. Some of Donald Trump's followers did not accept the outcome of the 2020 …
11. On 9 September 2001, the USA experienced the worst … attacks in its history.
12. After 9/11, national security has become a priority in American … policy.

A Shaping the USA

1 Reading for detail → SB, pp. 90–92

In the following statements some information is incorrect. Find the wrong details, underline them and rewrite the sentence with the correct information.

1. Miranda's version of the play features classical music and a traditional cast.

2. Hamilton and Washington work together to support British rule and stop the American Revolution.

3. After independence, Washington doesn't agree with Hamilton that America should act with its own interests in mind.

4. Hamilton is charitable and wants the people of America to be involved in developing its economic and foreign policy.

5. Hamilton is driven by money and excitement.

6. American patriots encouraged ambition.

7. Miranda's play glorifies ambition and doesn't show any of its negative sides.

2 Analysing a review

a Read the review of *Hamilton* and answer the questions using keywords.

***Hamilton:* An American musical** *by Lin-Manuel Miranda*

I've long been a die-hard *Hamilton* fan – I've been listening to the soundtrack on repeat ever since I saw the show on Broadway back in 2016. I was so lucky to win a ticket – 46 lottery tickets are offered every day, and I was one of around 10,000 people who entered each day!

Part of *Hamilton*'s charm is the clever use of hip-hop and rap influences to tell Hamilton's story. In 2009 I watched Miranda perform the opening number for an audience, including the Obamas, at the White House Poetry Jam. He explained that he was working on a hip-hop album about the life of someone he thought embodied hip-hop. When he announced that that person was Alexander Hamilton, the audience laughed. The idea is a little crazy.

Apparently, Miranda took a biography of Alexander Hamilton on holiday and as he was reading, he became convinced of the similarities between Hamilton and modern-day hip-hop stars. Hamilton was very good at putting words together. He wrote his way into Washington's good graces, then into trouble with other Founding Fathers, and didn't know when to stop writing. When Miranda read that Hamilton wrote under the pen name, 'Publius', he immediately thought that that was like his emcee – you know, a rapper's alternative title!

Almost all of *Hamilton* is sung through – like an opera. Cabinet debates are turned into rap battles. The music and lyrics come at you so fast. I read that if *Hamilton* were performed at the same speed as other Broadway musicals, it would be over six hours long.

Every time I listened to the soundtrack, I discovered something new. I knew very little about that period of history, and I wasn't expecting to enjoy a musical about political, economic and racial history, but what's so compelling about *Hamilton* is that it also offers commentary on the racial and cultural politics of the US today.

★★★★★ Maddie, Massachusetts

1. How did Miranda present his idea at the White House Poetry Jam?

____

____

2. Which similarities did Miranda see between Alexander Hamilton and modern hip-hop stars? Name two.

____

3. Which qualities of the musical did Maddie like? Name three.

____

____

b Say whether you would like to watch the musical *Hamilton*. Give reasons.

____

3 Focus on grammar

a Participle clauses are common in written English because they allow us to include information without making long or complicated sentences. They can be used to shorten both active and passive sentences or to join two sentences. Compare these sentences.

Longer sentence with relative clause:
Miranda's masterpiece, which was inspired by Ron Chernow's 2004 biography, features a hip-hop soundtrack.

Shorter sentence with participle clause:
Inspired by Ron Chernow's 2004 biography, Miranda's masterpiece features a hip-hop soundtrack.

Alexander Hamilton

b Underline the past participles in these sentences from the text.

1. "Born a nobody on the British-ruled island of Nevis, Hamilton became a romantic polymath who fought wars and duels [...]." (ll.10–13)
2. "In a society built on family labour, ambition often seemed useless as well as dangerous." (ll.92–94)
3. "Inspired by Ron Chernow's 2004 biography, Miranda's masterpiece features a hip-hop soundtrack, a multiracial cast and powerful arguments, in theatrical form, for a more inclusive America." (ll.16–20)

c Rewrite the first two sentences in exercise b in a longer form using relative clauses.

d Rewrite the following sentences in a shorter form, using participle clauses.

1. Alexander Hamilton, who was chosen by George Washington to become the first secretary of the treasury of the USA, later founded the country's first central bank.
2. Alexander Hamilton's youngest son, who was born a year after his oldest brother had been killed in a duel, was named Philip after this brother.
3. Hamilton, who was badly wounded in a duel, died before he even turned 50.
4. As a young man, Hamilton, who was tired of Nevis, emigrated to the USA to get an education.
5. On Nevis, Hamilton, who was raised by unmarried parents, was not allowed into education.

B Dreaming the American Dream

1 Focus on grammar → SB, pp. 94–95

A journalist interviews Abdi about his first months in the US. Complete the questions and answers.

Abdi, how ____________ 1 (to get into) the US?

I ________ 2 (to be) lucky and I ____________ 3 (to gain entry) through the annual visa lottery.

Why ____________ 4 (to want) to live in the US?

There ________ 5 (to be) a civil war in Somalia, my home country.

Do you remember how life in the US ____________ 6 (to feel) at the beginning?

It ________ 7 (to be) not easy at all. I ____________ 8 (to work hard) in a low-paid job and ____________ 9 (to experience) racism.

________ 10 (to be) your religion a problem to your work colleagues?

Well, maybe not a problem, but they ____________ 11 (to make fun of) me. I ____________ 12 (to tell) them that I am Muslim and therefore I have to pray five times a day. They ____________ 13 (to not know) that there are Muslims in Africa. They ____________ 14 (to think) that all Muslims look like Osama bin Laden.

You ____________ 15 (to mention) racism. How ____________ 16 (to experience) that?

My colleagues would ask to borrow money from me, but they never ____________ 17 (to pay sb back). Then my things ____________ 18 (to start) to disappear.

What ____________ 19 (to do)?

I ____________ 20 (to talk to) my boss but he said he couldn't do anything. Then one day I ____________ 21 (to find) my hard hat in the back of a colleague's pickup truck. The same guys I'd been working with for months – and when I ____________ 22 (to ask), they said nothing!

How ____________ 23 (to feel)?

It was humiliating. It ____________ 24 (to feel) as if my American Dream was shrinking.

Do you remember when that feeling ____________ 25 (to change)?

Yes. It ____________ 26 (to feel) different when I ____________ 27 (to come home) in the evening. When I ____________ 28 (to get home), I took a shower, ____________ 29 (to change) and walked back toward Main Street to relax. People recognized me, ____________ 30 (to wave) and smiled. I ____________ 31 (to start) to feel like part of a community.

2 Writing a dialogue → SB, p. 97

Complete the dialogue using the following words and phrases in the correct form and tense. There are more gaps than words and phrases, so you need to use your own ideas too.

backbreaking work | great news | housemaid | less than minimum wage | to afford | to deport | to discover | to earn | to expect a baby | to harvest produce | to make ends meet | to worry | to relate to people | to stay at home | to understand sb's religion and habits | to work legally | to win a Green Card in the lottery | to raise a child | US citizenship

Aarna: Abdi, you're so lucky you can ____ 1. For us it's much harder. A major fear of ours is ____ 2.

Abdi: Yes, I know. I'm very grateful that I ____ 3. I'm sorry that you have to ____ 4. What about your ____ 5? How much ____ 6?

Aarna: Well, I work as ____ 7 and Kabir ____ 8. It's ____ 9 and we ____ 10. Before we came here, we dreamt of ____ 11. Now I sometimes wonder whether we ____ 12.

Abdi: Before I left Somalia, I also dreamt of ____ 13. And what have I found here? I have a job and the pay is acceptable, but I find it hard ____ 14. They don't seem to ____ 15.

Aarna: I guess, we all have ____ 16. And I ____ 17. Normally, this would be great news, but I don't know ____ 18. We can't even ____ 19.

Abdi: Congratulations! I hope ____ 20. At least your child will ____ 21. I wish you all the best. Let's hope the situation of ____ 22.

A17 3 Listening: Forward Thinking: DREAMers → SB, p. 97

Answer the following questions in keywords.

1. What is Aiza Kaleb's profession? ____
2. What is the immigration status of people called DREAMers? ____
3. What can DREAMers do under DACA? Name three aspects. ____
4. What is Juanita's job and where does she work? ____
5. Why does Carlos' brother have US citizenship? ____
6. How does the US system profit from DREAMers? ____
7. What does Isabella say makes her a typical American? Name two aspects. ____

Analysing style, tone and register → SB, p. 98

1 Read the text blocks for starting and ending a speech on the topic "The United States of innovation" at a school event on Fourth of July. There will be friends and family there, but also teachers, the school's principal and the town mayor. Decide on the style, tone and register, and whether or not they are suitable for the occasion. Fill in the table below.

A Ms. Mayor, Mr. Principal, ladies and gentlemen,
The topic I was asked to talk about today is "The United States of innovation". The USA is no longer the leading country in innovation, as it was in 2007. In the Global Innovation Index of 2021, the USA is ranked third after Switzerland and Sweden. The ranking is based on the number of patents that have been filed internationally and on the scientific publishing activity.

B Ms. Mayor, Mr. Principal, ladies and gentlemen, fellow students, friends and family,
I am honoured to have been asked to speak here today. July Fourth is a day of celebration. And I would like to invite you to follow me in some thoughts on what we can celebrate on this day, the birthday of our beloved nation. Because although we are facing some serious problems, there is still so much there that we can be proud of. Just think of the amazing power of innovation that has been characteristic of the USA from its early days, and is continuing to do so today and into the future.

C So, I still think the USA is right up there, although China's getting pretty big too, isn't it? But no worries, with Bezos and the guys going to space and stuff, I don't think China's got a chance!

D The list of outstanding innovators in the USA could be continued forever. Let me conclude by saying this: Yes, the USA has its problems. And yes, we are facing major global challenges. But if we channel the innovative energy exemplified by the names I mentioned, into working towards solving those issues, and if innovations are not just thought of for profit, but for the sake of humanity, then the USA can make a valuable contribution.

	Style	Tone	Register	Suitability
A				
B				
C				
D				

2 Complete the extract of the main part of the speech with the following words and phrases.

assembly line | Bill Gates and Steve Jobs | car manufacturing | continuation | leading country | innovation and enterprising spirit | IT | transport in the future | more efficient | Tesla and SpaceX

To illustrate this, I would like to talk about some examples of ______________________ 1. To begin with, let us look back in history. In 1913, Henry Ford invented the ______________ 2 which revolutionised not only ______________________ 3 but made the entire production process faster and ______________________ 4. Then there is, of course, the huge realm of __________ 5. ______________________ 6 are just two very prominent names from among thousands of innovative people who have made the USA the ______________________ 7 in this field. And last but not least, I would like to mention Elon Musk, who is also an example of the ______________ 8 of innovative spirit in the USA. ______________________ 9 are his two best-known enterprises and their inventions may change ______________________ 10 fundamentally.

C Space and innovation

A18 1 Listening: The space race

Listen to the lecture on the original space race. Complete the table noting down the missing dates and information.

Date	USA	Soviet Union
October 1957		
		second satellite (Sputnik 2); first living being in space: dog (called Laika), does not survive
1958		
	satellites take pictures of Earth and far side of the moon	
1960		
1961		
		first man in space: Juri Gagarin; orbits Earth once
		first woman in space: Valentina Vladimirovna Tereshkova; orbits Earth 48 times
July 1969		

2 Focus on analysis → SB, pp. 99–101

Find one example of each of the following stylistic devices in the text and take notes on the effect they have on the reader.

Stylistic device	Example	Effect on the reader
1. metaphor		
2. contrast		
3. open question		
4. metonymy		

D The USA and the world

1 Focus on analysis → SB, pp.102–104

a Underline the correct options to complete the explanation of the quotation by Thomas Jefferson.

In the year 1801, in his first inaugural address Thomas Jefferson said the famous words "Peace, commerce, and honest friendship with all nations, entangling alliances with none." What he meant was that the USA should have **close and positive / positive but distanced** relationships with other countries and **should / should not** get involved in the conflicts and affairs of other countries. His position exemplifies an **interventionist / isolationist** attitude towards the USA's role in the world.

b Decide if the following quotations from Joe Biden's speech support or contradict Jefferson's message. Write S (= support) or C (= contradict) in the boxes. Give reasons.

1. ☐ "[…] engaging our adversaries and our competitors diplomatically […]" (ll. 55–56)

____

2. ☐ "[…] I've spoken with the leaders of many of our closest friends […] to begin reforming the habits of cooperation and rebuilding the muscle of democratic alliances […]" (ll. 41–47)

____

3. ☐ "[…] the United States and Russia agreed to extend the new START treaty […] safeguarding nuclear stability." (ll. 59–63)

____

4. ☐ "[…] standing shoulder to shoulder with our allies and key partners […]" (ll. 52–53)

____

5. ☐ "When we invest in economic development of countries, we create new markets for our products […]" (ll. 121–123)

____

c Complete the comparison of Jefferson's quotation with Biden's speech using the following words and phrases. There are two words or phrases you do not need.

allies | climate crisis | commerical interest | defense | democracy and freedom | echoes | peace | diplomatic relations | former alliances | isolationism | interventionism | markets | nuclear weapons

In his quotation, Thomas Jefferson clearly expresses a position of _______________ 1. Joe Biden _______________ 2 a few of the aspects touched upon by Jefferson: he mentions _______________ 3 in other countries which he sees as potential _______________ 4 for American products and he plans to form _______________ 5 with the USA's opponents. He also wants to cooperate with Russia on avoiding the danger of _______________ 6. In this way, Biden is pursuing _______________ 7 and an interest in commerce with countries that are not _______________ 8 of the USA. However, Biden stresses that he is planning to strengthen _______________ 9 and that he wants the USA to take an active role in the world, defending _______________ 10. Biden, thus, is clearly in support of _______________ 11.

1 Lesen und Schreiben → SB, pp. 110–111

1 Writing a summary

a Look at the following line numbers and read those passages. What example of division in the history of the USA does each of the passages refer to? Note down keywords.

1. ll. 17–36: "President-elect Joe Biden […] the U.S. Capitol in Washington D.C."

   ____
   ____
   ____
   ____

2. ll. 56–65: "The 18th century was […] if the other guy is elected."

   ____
   ____

3. ll. 72–82: "Or the Civil War […] fighting against people over a president, […]."

   ____
   ____

4. ll. 98–111: "As President-elect […] not just the people who voted for him? […]"

   ____
   ____

b Complete the summary below using information from the text.

The newspaper comment "Americans reflect on a divided nation: 'This doesn't feel like America'", published in *CBS News* in 2021, mentions examples of ____________ 1 from earlier to very recent events.

In the 18th century, people feared that the government would take their ____________ 2, and that the country was going to collapse if the candidate they did not support ____________ 3.

In the 19th century, the USA experienced ____________ 4 between the North and the South, in which ____________ 5 fought each other. In 2020, the country was divided over ____________ 6 which, according to a person quoted in the text, were supported by Joe Biden. This gave rise to doubts whether he ____________ 7.

On 6 January 2021, a mob stormed the Capitol Building in protest of ____________ 8 – an act which threatened the tradition of ____________ 9.

2 Words matter

a Find words in the text that belong to the same thematic field as the following, including both synonyms and antonyms. Give line numbers.

1. divided (l. 1): ______________________

   ____

2. turmoil (l. 10): ______________________
3. threat (l. 25): ______________________
4. to collapse (l. 51): ______________________

b Find words in the text to form collocations with the words in the left column of table below. Then add a German translation of each collocation.

Collocation	German translation
1. fellow	
2. peaceful	
3. turbulent	
4. conspiracy	
5. usurpation	

3 Writing a blog post

To prepare your blog post, take notes on the following developments in American history and the ways in which they are examples of division in the USA.

1. The Civil Rights Movement

   ____

   ____

   ____

   ____

2. #BlackLivesMatter

   ____

   ____

3. #MarchForOurLives / #NeverAgain

   ____

   ____

   ____

4. Abortion legislation

   ____

   ____

   ____

2 Hörverstehen → SB, p. 111

A19

Listen to the radio report and choose the correct answer from the options (a, b or c) given below. There is only one correct answer.

1. When asked whether a nationality unites the USA, a boy scout answers that the country is held together by …
   a ☐ shared values.
   b ☐ religious beliefs.
   c ☐ a set of national characteristics.
2. According to Shadi Hamid, becoming American is …
   a ☐ very difficult for immigrants.
   b ☐ possible for anyone who immigrates to the USA.
   c ☐ more difficult than becoming German or Swedish.
3. Professor Lynn Itagaki states that …
   a ☐ the civil religion in the USA creates harmony.
   b ☐ everyone is equal under the USA's civil religion.
   c ☐ certain groups do not have a part in the civil religion of the USA.
4. According to Shadi Hamid, the fact that many Founding Fathers were slaveholders …
   a ☐ means that the founding documents have lost their value.
   b ☐ should not mean that the founding documents have lost their value.
   c ☐ should mean that the value of the founding documents should be reconsidered.
5. Myles Werntz's opinion on the use of Christian language in political rhetoric is that it …
   a ☐ can also transport basic moral values.
   b ☐ should not be allowed after 6 January 2021.
   c ☐ is dangerous and should be outlawed altogether.
6. Nicole Sarty teaches her students about …
   a ☐ the basics of the US government.
   b ☐ waves of immigration in US history.
   c ☐ the importance of the USA in the world.
7. Katie Munn showed Nicole Sarty's students …
   a ☐ the National Archives.
   b ☐ the Charters of Freedom in an online tour.
   c ☐ documents about the struggle for women's suffrage.
8. Philip Gorski believes that in the USA's civil religion …
   a ☐ the idea of 'saints' is no longer meaningful.
   b ☐ the Founding Fathers should be replaced as 'saints' by more diverse people.
   c ☐ a more diverse group of people should be added as 'saints' to the Founding Fathers.

Hörverstehen

A20 1 Listening for gist

Listen to five people talking about the region of the USA they come from. Match the following headings with the speakers (1–5). There is one heading you do not need.

A Bibles and jazz ☐
B Taking things slow ☐
C Living in the desert ☐
D The centre of learning ☐
E Progressive but pricey ☐
F Democracy in paradise ☐

A20 2 Listening for detail

a Listen again and take notes on the five different regions in the table below.

New England	
The South	
The West Coast	
The Midwest	
Guam	

b Listen again and answer the following questions in keywords.

1. Which states are part of the New England region? Name three.
   ___
2. Which major universities are based in the New England region? Name two.
   ___
3. Which characteristics set the South apart from the rest of the US? Name two.
   ___
4. What are the main appeals of Florida? Name two.
   ___
5. What is the main news regarding California?
   ___
6. Which language used to be common in the Midwest? What is its status today?
   ___
7. Why is Guam seen as the place "where America's day begins"?
   ___
8. What are the downsides of living in Guam? Name three.
   ___

3 Pre-listening

Think about the ways a person can feed into their nation's culture as they grow up. Note down your ideas.

____

____

A21 4 Listening for gist

Listen to the podcast in which a young man talks about Northern Irish and British identities. Choose the correct answer from the options (a, b or c) given below. There is only one correct answer.

1. Decide which of the following summaries best suits how Jordan describes his identity.
   - a ☐ He is a mix of being British and Irish.
   - b ☐ After moving to England, he realised that he felt truly British.
   - c ☐ While he identifies primarily as Northern Irish, he also feels British in a way.
2. Over time, identity in Northern Ireland has ...
   - a ☐ become more flexible.
   - b ☐ become more restricted.
   - c ☐ drifted more towards being British.
3. Jordan has grown up mainly ...
   - a ☐ with British cultural elements.
   - b ☐ isolated from British influences.
   - c ☐ with strong Irish cultural and media influence.

A21 5 Listening for detail

Listen again and answer the following questions in keywords.

1. What can you infer about how people in Southern England view Northern Irish identity?

   ____

2. According to Jordan, which characteristics are typically Northern Irish? Name two.

   ____

3. What does Jordan say can lead to misunderstandings between the Northern Irish and people from Southern Ireland and Southern England? Why is this the case?

   ____

   ____

6 Post-listening

Write down your thoughts on the statement "Your passport is what defines your culture".

____

____

____

____

The UK and its people

1 Listening: A United Kingdom → SB, p.113

a Before you listen, match these words and phrases from the listening text to their definitions.

1. constituency
2. cultural reference
3. devolved
4. reunification
5. rivalry
6. to have sth in common
7. to set sth apart
8. with good grace

A transferred from central government to regional administration
B to make sth different from sth else
C in a willing and pleasant way
D pointing at sth that relates to the culture of a country or region
E joining parts of a country so they form a political unit again
F to share the same interests or ideas
G people or institutions competing for the same thing
H a district that elects its own representative to parliament

1	2	3	4	5	6	7	8

A22 **b** Listen to the recording and answer the questions in keywords.

1. Which countries make up the United Kingdom?

____

2. What reasons does Sura give that show that the UK is united? Name two aspects.

____

3. According to John, why is the UK politically disunited?

____

4. In Dave's and Lottie's opinion, what do people in the UK share? Name four aspects.

____

2 Working with a cartoon

Complete the text with the following words.

border control | commenting | culture | devolved | sign | identities | majority | movement | proposed | referendum

The cartoon by Ron McGeary shows a serious looking UK ______________ 1 officer standing beside a large ______________ 2 that reads "You are now entering the Disunited Kingdom". It is ______________ 3 on the fact that although the UK is called 'united', Northern Ireland, Scotland and Wales have ______________ 4 parliaments. While these nations share a language and a ______________ 5 with England, they each have distinct ______________ 6 . Also, there is an independence ______________ 7 , particularly in Scotland, where the SNP has a ______________ 8 . In the 2014 Scottish independence ______________ 9 , 44.7% answered 'Yes' and 55.3% 'No'. A second referendum has been ______________ 10 after the UK voted to leave the EU in 2016.

A English and its regional varieties

1 Crossword puzzle: Regional dialects in the UK → SB, pp. 114–115

Complete the crossword puzzle with adjectives and adverbs from the text.

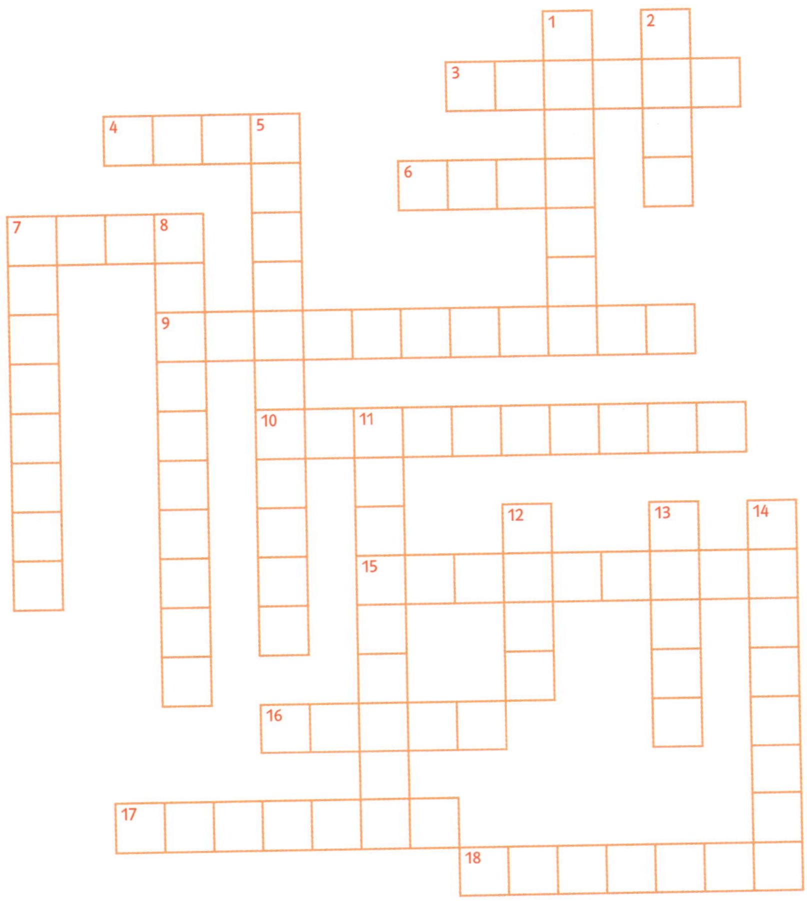

Across (→)

3. one of a kind, highly special
4. able to make good decisions based on knowledge and experience
6. very uncommon
7. characteristic of a high social class
9. very attractive, impressive
10. silly, unreasonable
15. typical of a child
16. fancy, flashy
17. unlimited
18. not average

Down (↓)

1. various kinds of sth
2. sweet, lovable
5. seemingly bigger, better or worse than sth really is
7. satisfying, fulfilling
8. consisting of the same things or people
11. tasty
12. made to look real
13. not serious, unimportant
14. coming from a certain part of a country

2 Reading for detail → SB, pp. 114–115

Read the text and answer the questions in keywords. Give line numbers to support your answers.

1. Which four expressions from regional dialects have recently been included in the OED?

 ____

2. Why do some Britons take 'accent softening' lessons?

 ____

3. According to the author, what prompted half the country to embrace regional variation?

 ____

4. What is 'upspeak'?

 ____

5. What impact did the inclusion of regional terms in the OED have?

 ____

3 Focus on analysis → SB, pp. 114–116

a Examine whether the adverbs and adjectives from the text listed in the table below have a positive (+) or negative (–) connotation and rephrase the expressions. Use a bilingual dictionary to help you.

Adverb / adjective	Connotation +/–	Rephrase in your own words
1. a rare piece of happy news (l. 4)		
2. delicious word (l. 12)		
3. wise custodians (l. 23)		
4. actively embracing (l. 24)		
5. cute accents (l. 54)		
6. pronounce it properly (l. 62)		
7. regional idiosyncrasies (l. 78)		
8. homogenous tone (l. 80)		
9. sounded ridiculous and infantile (l. 91)		
10. fake glottal stops (l. 93)		
11. diverse glory (l. 108)		
12. endless enthusiasm (l. 111)		

b Select three expressions from the table and explain the effect of the adverbs and adjectives.

____

____

____

____

____

____

B National identity

1 Talking about British identity → SB, pp. 117–119

Create a word web exploring different aspects of what might be considered to be British. Use the pictures in your book and the words below to give you some ideas.

cities | ethnic groups | films and series | food | landscape | literature | monarchy | pop music | sights | sport

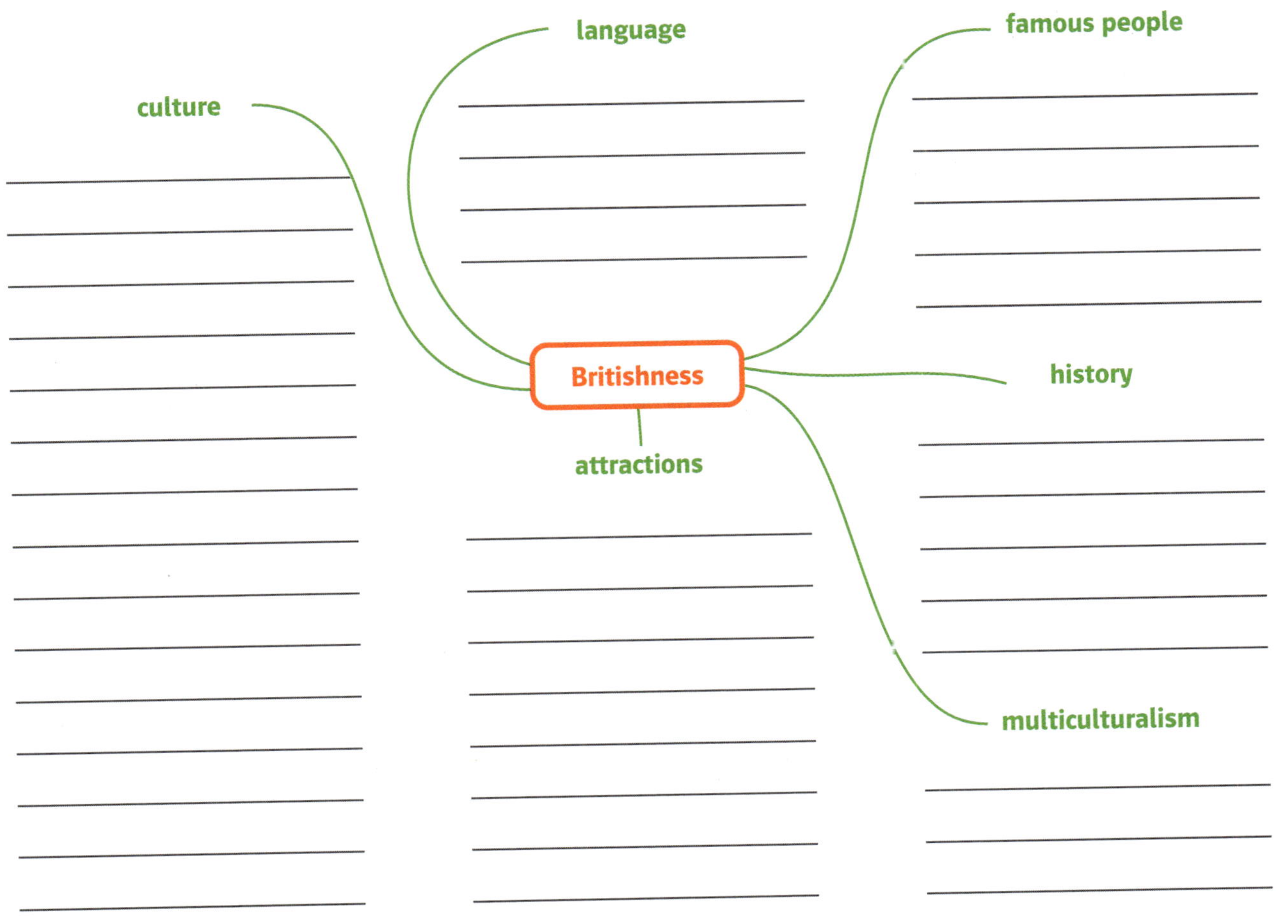

2 Reading for detail → SB, pp. 117–119

Decide whether the following statements are true or false. Give line numbers to support your answers and correct the false statements.

Statement	True	False
1. The winner of *The Great British Bake Off* gets a substantial cash prize.		
2. Mary Berry is one of the judges on the show.		
3. The author of the text is from the US.		
4. Only one of the finalists has written a cookbook.		
5. The show celebrates British culture while including elements from other cultures.		

3 Writing a blog post → SB, pp. 117–118, p. 120

To help you prepare your blog post, explain what the following quotes from the two texts say about how immigrants are accepted in the UK.

Quotes from "'The Great British Bake Off' Can Win Any Culture War"	Explanation
1. "It is a place where heritage and culture stand proud, enriched but not diluted by the traditions of immigrants." (ll. 2–4)	everyone is includet
2. "An island of confident identity in a fractured and contentious world, it celebrates cosmopolitan curiosity and deep-rooted traditions, local custom and diverse origins." (ll. 7–12)	
3. "The welcoming atmosphere is 'so different from the picture Brexit painted, that the British want their nation back and that they want us out,' Chetna Makan, a 2014 contestant who moved to the U.K. from Mumbai, told the New York Times." (ll. 45–50)	Strengh in society
4. "GBBO, as fans refer to it, rejects the choice between openness and national identity." (ll. 65–66)	openness
5. "[…] the show welcomes global citizens and the flavors they introduce." (ll. 94–95)	everyone has a chanc
6. "A cooking contest alone can't mend a society's divisions, of course. But the success of this one suggests they may not be as deep as they seem." (ll. 134–137)	Excaptance

Quotes from "Nadiya Hussein: 'I want to blend in. But the truth is, I'm never going to blend in'"	Explanation
1. "'I want to blend in. But the truth is, I'm never going to blend in'" (ll. 1–2)	To fit in / integrate is very dificult or impossible
2. "[…] she transformed from a shy, uncertain home cook into a Great British Bake Off winner, the best-loved winner in the history of the series." (ll. 8–11)	She turned r
3. "[…] there's no space [in the industry] for someone like me. I've learned that if I don't create that space, who will?" (ll. 28–30)	
4. "I get bits of my books ripped apart because, am I English enough to be writing these things?" (ll. 39–41)	
5. "Because I'm a daughter of an immigrant, because I am bilingual, because I'm a Muslim, because I'm a brown woman, because I don't fit into that industry or fit into these worlds, I'm constantly up for scrutiny." (ll. 49–54)	

Working with maps

→ SB, pp.121–122

1 Look at the map of Scotland and sum up what it is about.

___

___

___

Projected population change, 2018 to 2028 in Scotland

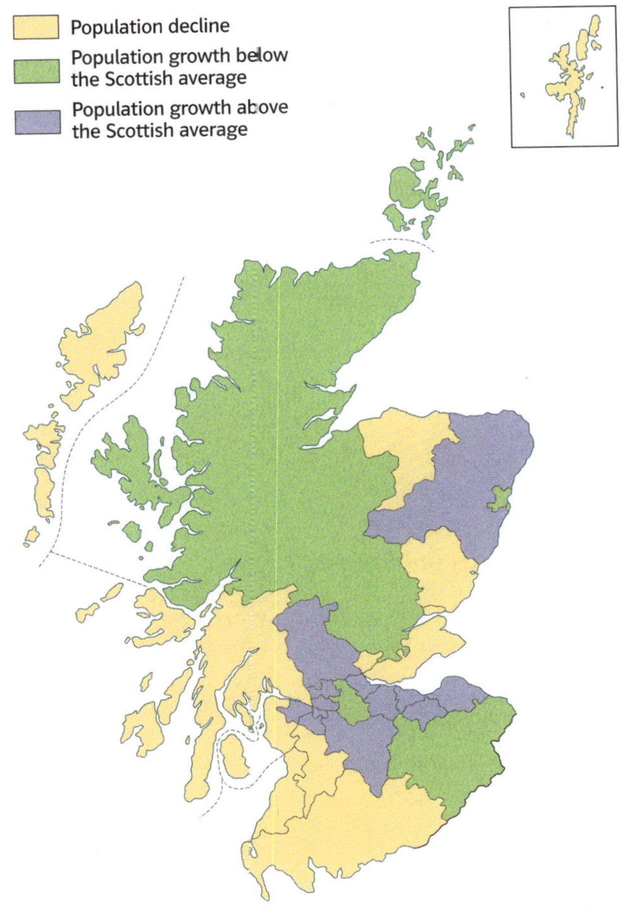

Source: National Records of Scotland, 2018

2 Use the following words and numbers to complete the description and analysis of the map. There are two words or numbers you do not need.

2018 | 2022 | 2028 | above average | area | birth rate | Central Belt | country | deaths | decrease | depicts | expected | green | key | light purple | migration | population change | regions | rise | shaded | south-west | spectrum | stretches | urban areas | west | yellow

The map shows the projected ___ ___ 1 in different parts of Scotland in the period between ___ 2 and ___ 3. Scotland is the second largest ___ 4 in the United Kingdom, covering an ___ 5 of 78,782 km².

On the map, the different ___ 6 of Scotland are ___ 7 according to their ___ 8 population development. The ___ 9 states that regions ___ 10 in colour are going to have a ___ 11 in their population, whereas regions coloured in ___ 12 are going to have a ___ 13 which is lower than average. At the other end of the ___ 14, parts of north-east and central Scotland are marked in ___ 15, indicating that the population in these areas is going to see an ___ 16 increase. The map predicts that the population in the regions located in the so-called ___ 17 – an area that ___ 18 from the east to the ___ 19 between the cities of Edinburgh and Glasgow, including the large towns of Paisley, Stirling, Falkirk, Perth and Dundee – as well as in other ___ 20 is going to grow. At the same time the population especially in the west and ___ 21 of Scotland will decrease.

The population growth in some parts of Scotland is likely to be caused by ___ 22 from within the UK and from other countries. Possible reasons for the decrease in the population in certain parts of the country might be a rising number of ___ 23 combined with a falling ___ 24.

C History from another perspective

1 Reading for detail → SB, pp. 123–125

Write keywords in the thought bubbles about Doris' possible feelings regarding her imminent escape from the United Kingdom of Great Ambossa.

AT FIRST

____

____

____

____

THEN

____

____

____

____

2 Focus on analysis → SB, pp. 123–125

Explain the following words and expressions used in the text to describe Chief Kaga Konata Katamba I and fill in the table. Use a bilingual dictionary to help you.

Quote	Explanation
1. "made his fortune in the import-export game, the notorious transatlantic slave run" (ll. 3–4)	
2. "absentee sugar baron" (l. 5)	
3. "part-time husband" (l. 5)	
4. "free-lance father" (l. 5)	
5. "retired decent human being" (l. 5)	
6. "sacked soul" (l. 6)	
7. "full-time anti-abolitionist" (l. 7)	

A23 3 Listening: Legacies of British slave ownership

Listen to the radio programme and match the headings with the names. There are two more headings than you need.

A Colonial roots
B Opposing views
C The British Empire
D Statues and history
E Educating the public
F Public and private spaces
G Using art to change meanings
H Opinions on the Rhodes statue

Name	Alexander	Fearne	Marcus	Millie	Niz	Olia
Heading						

D Food poverty in the UK

1 Words matter → SB, pp. 127–128

Match the following words and phrases from the text to the correct definitions.

1. affiliation
2. benefit system
3. deficit
4. digs
5. distribution
6. furlough scheme
7. hardship
8. plea
9. to exist on a knife's edge
10. vulnerable

A room(s) that you rent to live in
B sb's connection with a political party or religion
C a situation that is difficult or causes suffering
D the process of giving sth out to people
E government support for employers to pay wages
F easily hurt physically, mentally or emotionally
G money given by the state to unemployed or ill people
H living in an extremely challenging or a dangerous situation
I a serious emotional request for sth requiring action
J the amount of money which is spent more than received

2 Reading for detail → SB, pp. 127–129

Read the text and answer the following questions in keywords.

1. Who is Marcus Rashford and what is he campaigning against?
   ______
   ______
2. What was difficult about his mother's work situation while Marcus was growing up?
   ______
3. What helped Marcus' family to cope with their challenges? Name three aspects.
   ______
4. What is FareShare?
   ______
5. How many children in the UK are living in poverty?
   ______
6. What insights has Marcus gained from talking to parents? Name two aspects.
   ______
7. Why did parents like Marcus' depend on kids' clubs in the summer holidays? Name two reasons.
   ______
8. In his letter, what is Marcus asking MPs to do?
   ______

3 Focus on analysis → SB, pp. 127–129

Complete the table below with the missing quotes and effects of the stylistic devices on the reader.

Stylistic device	Quote	Effects on the reader
1. direct address		engages and involves the reader
2. enumeration	"Men, women, caregivers, are calling out for our help and we aren't listening." (ll. 114–116)	
3. repetition		convinces the reader of the importance
4. rhetorical question	"Political affiliations aside, can we not all agree that no child should be going to bed hungry?" (ll. 61–63)	
5. appeal		gives the text an authoritative edge; addresses the reader's emotions

4 Working with an infographic

Complete the sentences describing and analysing the infographic.

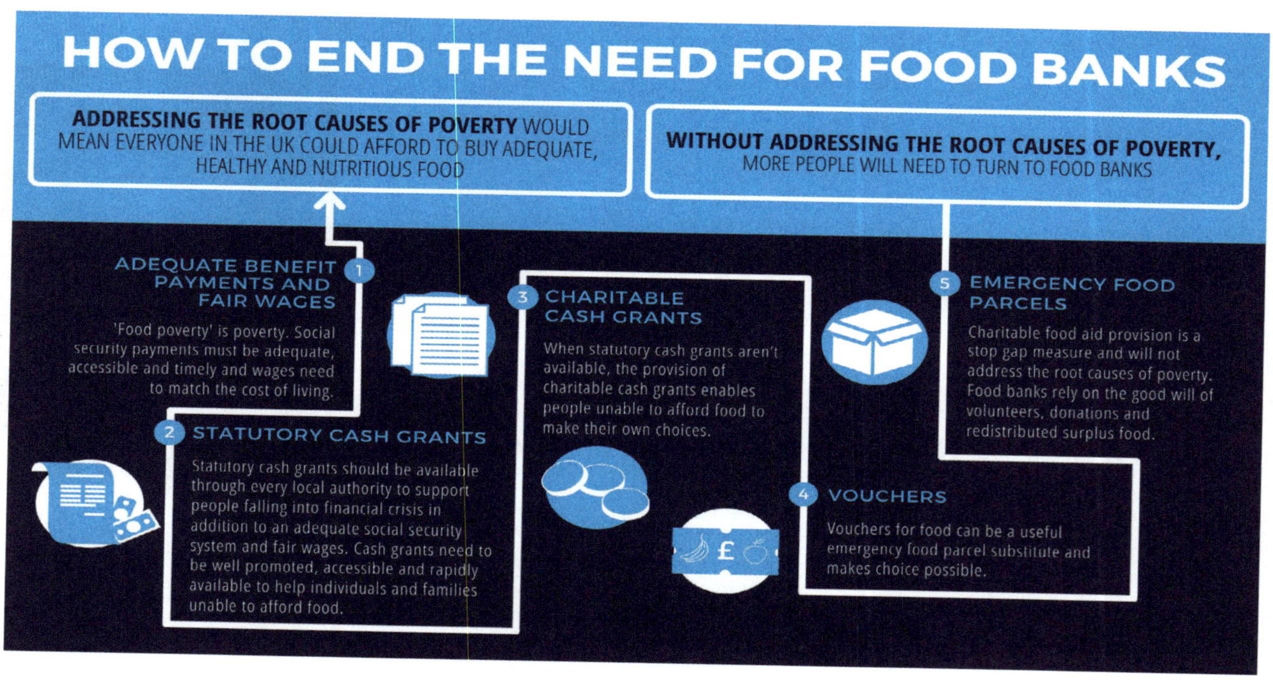

This infographic is titled ______________________ 1. The title is on a light blue background, while ______________________ 2. Following the numbers from five to one leads from a subheading at the top right which reads ______________________ 3 to another subheading ______________________ 4. According to the infographic, a solution to poverty would be ______________________ 5. The infographic draws attention to the fact ______________________ 6.

1 Lesen und Schreiben → SB, pp. 134–135

1 Words matter

Find the German translations to these words and phrases from the text and add a definition for each.

English	German	Definition
1. artistry		
2. athleticism		
3. exclusivity		
4. heritage		
5. outsized contribution		
6. squad		
7. tireless		
8. cemented		
9. geared towards sth		
10. shortlisted		
11. to pursue sth		
12. to remould sth		

2 Writing an email

a Read the text again and collect arguments that support the author's statement "diversity is making an outsized contribution to British culture" (ll. 58–59). Note down examples for each heading in the table below. Add your own ideas too.

Cultural power	Openness to diversity	United in admiration for ...

b Explain what the author refers to when he says "Diversity is what makes Britain's culture great. But recently it has felt as though we have lost sight of this self-evident truth." (ll. 87–89)

c Use your notes in exercises a and b to complete the letter to the editor in which you comment on the author's statement that "diversity is making an outsized contribution to British culture" (ll. 58–59).

Dear Editor, ______________________

I have just read the article ______________________ ← Refer to the article and where it was published.

____

I am writing to ______________________ ← State your reason for writing.

____

I couldn't agree more that ______________________ ← Use your notes to explain your viewpoint.

____

____

____

____

____

____

____

____

______________________ ← Finish by summing up your main point in one memorable sentence.

It is diversity that ______________________

____

______________________ ← Give your name and the place where you live.

____

2 Hörverstehen → SB, p. 135

1 Words matter

Before you listen, match the following words from the listening text with their corresponding definitions.

1. to advocate sth
2. arbitrary
3. complicit in sth
4. to erase sth
5. to grapple with sth
6. intimidated by sth
7. proceeds
8. to reconcile sth
9. to skip over sth
10. spine-chilling

A to settle or resolve a conflict or situation
B to remove or destroy sth completely
C very frightening
D to feel scared because you are not confident in a situation
E to not do sth that you usually do or should do
F to support sth publicly
G based on chance rather than planning or reason
H involved or knowing about sth that is wrong or illegal
I the money received from sth
J to make a big effort to tackle sth

1	2	3	4	5	6	7	8	9	10

2 Listening: Loose Ends

A24 **a** Listen to the first part of the interview with Afua Hirsch and choose the correct answer(s) from the options (a, b or c) given below. There can be more than one correct answer.

1. In her podcast, Afua Hirsch talks to …
   - a ☐ a lawyer, an author, a journalist and a broadcaster.
   - b ☐ families who made a fortune in the British Empire.
   - c ☐ well-known people with families connected to the British Empire.
2. Afua Hirsch believes that …
   - a ☐ most families have had tragic experiences of the British Empire.
   - b ☐ the British Empire is the key to understanding the British nation.
   - c ☐ the history of all families in Britain has been influenced by the British Empire in some way.
3. Anita Rani tells stories about the experience of …
   - a ☐ her grandparents' generation of the separation between Pakistan and India.
   - b ☐ the transfer of Hong Kong, which was the last part of the British Empire, to China.
   - c ☐ her ancestors' involvement in the independence movement and war against the French in Algeria.
4. Afua Hirsch believes that …
   - a ☐ Britons are embracing their society's rich history.
   - b ☐ the British do not talk enough about the way and reasons why the British Empire collapsed.
   - c ☐ Britain's sense of faded glory plays a key role regarding the country's place in the world today.

A25 **b** Listen to the second part of the interview and choose the correct answer from the options (a, b or c) given below. There is only one correct answer.

1. At school, Afua Hirsch learned about …
   - a ☐ the British Empire.
   - b ☐ the Iron Age and the Romans.
   - c ☐ World War II and the Tudor period.
2. In a column she wrote in *The Guardian*, Afua Hirsch …
   - a ☐ proposed to remove the statue of Nelson in Trafalgar Square.
   - b ☐ advocated a better understanding of the role played by figures such as Nelson.
   - c ☐ was being deliberately provocative in her choice of the headline for the column.
3. Afua Hirsch would like …
   - a ☐ people to be deprived of engaging with history more meaningfully.
   - b ☐ history teachers to skip over the entire period of British colonialism.
   - c ☐ to help people understand the parts of history that have been whitewashed.
4. Winsome Pinnock …
   - a ☐ explores the destruction of history in her play on Radio Three.
   - b ☐ wrote a theatre play about Britain's historic role in the slave trade.
   - c ☐ is one of the people Afua Hirsch presents and talks to in her podcast.

Diverse identities

1 Talking about diverse identities

Write down a caption and description for each picture. Use the following words and phrases to help you.

diversity | traditional role models | individuality | gender | stereotype | non-binary | heterosexuality | homosexuality | clothing | LGBT+ | understanding | transgender | orientation | uncommon | feel empowered | equal | inclusive | inclusion | transition (into) | wedding | physical disability | free climbing | proud | prothesis | get married | bride and groom

A ____________________

B ____________________

C ____

____

____

____

____

D ____

____

____

____

____

A26 **2 Listening: Forward Thinking: Diversity in society** → SB, pp. 136–137

Listen to the podcast and choose the correct answer from the options (a, b or c) given below. There is only one correct answer.

1. Where did the first immigrants who arrived in the United States tend to live?
   - a ☐ in the middle of society
   - b ☐ in ethnically diverse neighbourhoods
   - c ☐ with other immigrants from their home country
2. The number of ethnic neighbourhoods today …
   - a ☐ is still high in most big cities.
   - b ☐ has decreased, although some still exist.
   - c ☐ is equal to the number of ethnically mixed neighbourhoods.
3. What did Alabama's state constitution forbid people from doing until the year 2000?
   - a ☐ marrying people of a different race
   - b ☐ marrying people from another state
   - c ☐ marrying people with a different social background
4. The Two-Spirit gender identity …
   - a ☐ is a cultural tradition in Canada.
   - b ☐ originated in Vancouver, Canada.
   - c ☐ is an additional gender in the culture of some Native American tribes.
5. How does Duane's cooperative include different groups?
   - a ☐ they add a plus symbol
   - b ☐ they ask for community support
   - c ☐ they continue to add new letters for new identities
6. What was the meaning of 'gay' in relation to gender in the 1970s?
   - a ☐ lesbian, gay or bisexual
   - b ☐ any diverse gender identity
   - c ☐ only what the mainstream was aware of

A Challenging identities

1 Reading for gist → SB, pp. 138–139

Match the headings with four sections from the excerpt of *The Vanishing Half*. Write down line numbers. There are more headings than you need.

A Passing over is dangerous ______
B The transformation ______
C The Founder's Day Dance ______
D White folks are fools ______
E What makes you free? ______
F Stella's experiments ______
G A definitive step ______
H The disguise ______

2 Reading for detail → SB, pp. 138–140

Read the text and answer the following questions.

1. Who is the first person who thinks that Stella is white?
______
2. What was extraordinary about Stella visiting the art museum on a Saturday?
______
3. What does Stella think is the secret to being white?
______
4. Where did Stella and Desiree run away to?
______
5. Why did Stella think she had a chance to get the job at Maison Blanche?
______
6. Why did Stella think she didn't have a chance to get the job at Maison Blanche?
______
7. What scared Stella most about getting the job?
______
8. What advantages did Stella have when she was with Blake?
______
9. Why didn't Stella want to reveal her true identity to Blake?
______
10. What did Desiree accuse Stella of doing?
______

3 Focus on analysis → SB, pp.138–140

Decide whether the excerpts indicate an inner or outer conflict Stella faces throughout her journey. Explain why.

Excerpt	Conflict	Explanation
1. "'But white folks can't tell', she said. 'Look at you – you just as redheaded as Father Cavanaugh. Why does he get to be white and you don't?'" (ll.10–12)		
2. "'You won't tell my mama, will you?'" (l.13)		
3. "[…] she'd gone to the South Louisiana Museum of Art on an ordinary Saturday morning, not Negro Day, and walked right up to the main entrance, not the side door where Negroes lined up in the alley." (ll.16–18)		
4. "She'd been daydreaming during her shift, thinking, again, about the morning she'd visited the museum as a white girl. […] She'd never felt so free." (ll.26–28)		
5. "Still, Desiree told her she had to apply." (l.32)		
6. "She almost said no. Told Desiree, forget it." (l.33)		
7. "She could become whichever woman she decided, whichever side of her face she tilted to the light." (ll.61–62)		

4 Working with a video → SB, p.141

Write a short review of the video. You can use the the following words and phrases to help you.

This video introduces us to … | The documentary portrays … | narrator | monologue | dialogue | interview | to enhance the mood | to distract from the message | powerful | rural setting | peaceful | authentic | direct | inspirational | relevant | resolute

B Diversity in gender

1 Reading for detail → SB, pp. 142–143

a Complete the word web with details about Santi, their mother and their brother and their actions with information from the text.

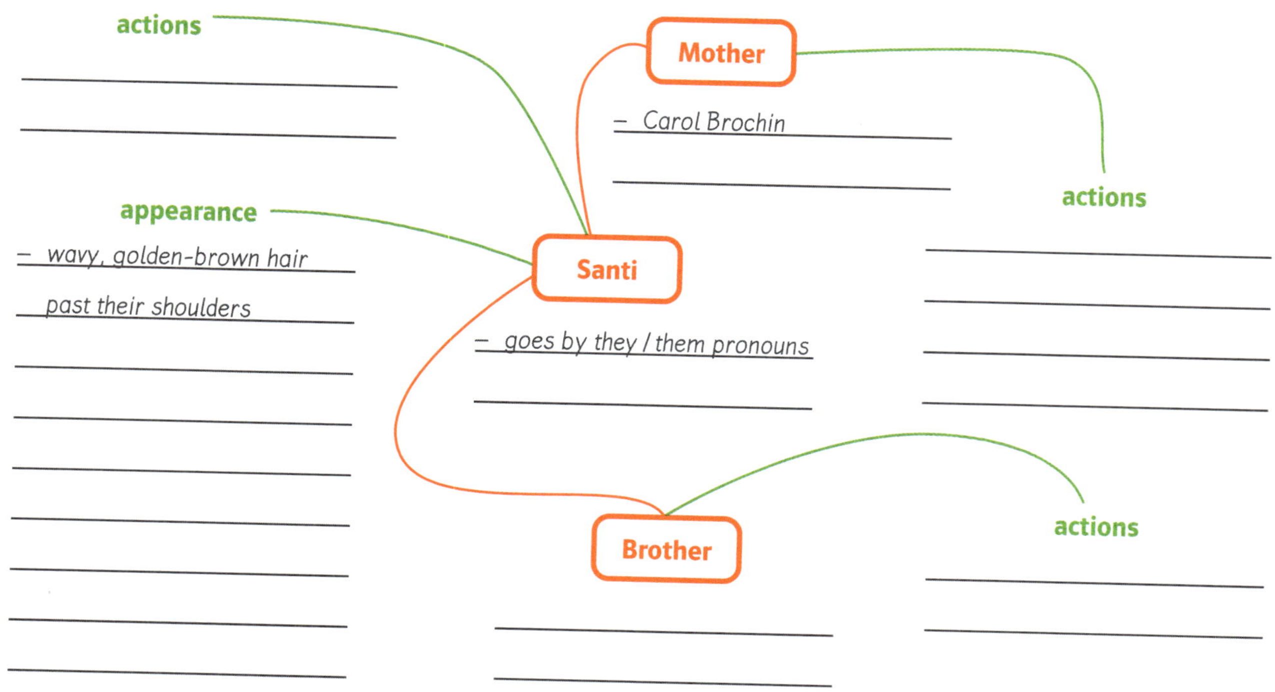

b List the things that happened to Santi at school.

c "Santi has had a long and sometimes painful journey" (ll. 27–28). Explain what Santi's mother means with this statement.

2 Focus on grammar

You want to tell your partner what Santi and Mrs Brochin say in the article. Change the sentences from direct speech into reported speech. Use the past tense and refer to Santi as using they / them.

1. "'It's sort of like treating me as a different species,' said Santi Ceballos […]." (ll. 5–7)
2. "'There's not only two genders!' Santi continues. 'Just let us be who we want to beeee …'" (ll. 12–14)
3. "'That's when I came out, kind of,' they said, smiling shyly." (ll. 61–62)

4. "'I tell my pre-service teachers, 'You have to be prepared. The kids are going to transition,' Brochin says." (ll. 33–36)

____

____

5. "'People often talk about it as, like, you come down the mountain and there's lots of tears and then you have to re-enter society,' she says." (ll. 65–69)

____

____

6. "'It caused a lot of dysmorphia and suicidal ideation,' Brochin recalls." (ll. 99–101)

____

3 Working with a cartoon

a Describe the cartoon.

____

____

____

____

____

____

____

____

____

____

____

"Oh, you'll love working here. Nobody treats you any differently just because of your age, race, or gender."

b Use the words to complete the analysis of the message of the cartoon.

enrichment | alike | monochrome | diversity | contradicts | irony | treated | appreciated

The cartoon uses ____________ 1 to show that there is no ____________ 2 in this company, and that is why you are not ____________ 3 differently. There are no differences – all of the people are ____________ 4. It ____________ 5 the idea that diversity is an ____________ 6. Multiculturalism is not ____________ 7 in this company, which can be seen as a ____________ 8 culture.

c State your opinion on the topic of the cartoon.

____

____

____

Talking about conditions → SB, p.145

1 Match the sentence parts to make conditional sentences about gender diversity.

1. If I had told my family earlier about my feelings,
2. There is a prejudice against diverse people,
3. Most young people will accept you
4. If you look back at history,
5. If people weren't declared a boy or girl at birth,
6. There would be fewer gender-related crimes

A if not enough is known about the topic.

B you will find a lot of different examples of gender diversity.

C if the issue were more accepted.

D they would have understood so much more about me.

E if you explain your feelings to them.

F it would perhaps be easier to explain diverse gender identities.

2 Fill in the blanks with the correct verb forms in brackets.

Depression sometimes feels like hell. But if I ________________ 1 (can), would I change what I've been through? No, I don't think I would change anything if I ________________ 2 (to be) completely honest with you. Don't get me wrong. I don't think depression is good. But I believe that if you ________________ 3 (to have) negative experiences, you should change them into something positive. I wouldn't have learned about the important things in life, like laughing, if I ________________ 4 (to not go) through times without laughter. If you tell people you suffer from depression, society ________________ 5 (to confront) you with social stigmas. That's a given. But you should still tell them. And these people will stand by you if they ________________ 6 (to be) real friends. If there's one thing that's extremely important to know, it's that you should not suffer in silence. If I hadn't shared my feelings and opened up, I definitely ________________ 7 (to not be) here today to share my story with you. Remember, you ________________ 8 (to find) yourself in a much better, happier place if you accept help and work hard at getting better – because it is work. If someone ________________ 9 (to ask) you for help, you would say yes, wouldn't you? So what's stopping you from asking?

3 Complete these conditional sentences with your own ideas.

1. If I moved to a different country, ________________________________
____
2. If society doesn't change its perspectives, ________________________
____
3. We would have achieved much more ______________________________
____
4. The world will become a better place ____________________________
____

C Two worlds?

1 Reading for gist → SB, pp. 146–148

a Decide which of the four scenes these sentences fit. Write the number of the scene in the right column.

Sentence	Scene
1. "I know you did, but I never asked you or Dad to do that for me."	_____
2. "That's a lot of different women to meet."	_____
3. "I wanted to tell Emily, but the moment never seemed right."	_____
4. "As a real Pakistani man, you should have one, Kumail."	_____
5. "Finding someone to marry is something I have to do on my own."	_____
6. "Was it a romantic meeting?"	_____
7. "Didn't your family put a lot of pressure on you to end the relationship?"	_____
8. "And I haven't told mom or dad yet. So don't say anything."	_____

b Complete the text with the following words and phrases.

back in Pakistan | better life | between | courage | expect | fulfil their wish | fallen in love | have sacrificed | introduce | love for her | mind of his own | misunderstanding | no intention | marrying | patiently

Kumail's parents ____________ 1 a lot for their son in order to offer him a ____________ 2 than they had in Pakistan. They believe that to repay them for this, Kumail should ____________ 3 that he marry a Pakistani girl. In order to 'help' him with this, they ____________ 4 him to numerous Pakistani women. But Kumail has a ____________ 5.

He ____________ 6 meets the Pakistani women that his mother invites to their house, but he has ____________ 7 of seeing them again or ____________ 8 any of them. However, Kumail also doesn't have the ____________ 9 to tell his parents that he has ____________ 10 with a white girl. When he finally does tell them about Emily and his ____________ 11, his mother throws him out of the family. There is a lot of ____________ 12 and miscommunication ____________ 13 Kumail and his parents. He thinks they are living like they are still ____________ 14 and ____________ 15 him to do the same.

2 Reading for detail → SB, pp. 146–148

Complete these sentences in your own words.

1. Naveed's advice for his brother Kumail is ____________________
2. In the first scene, Kumail believes that his mother ____________________
3. What makes Emily angriest in the second scene is ____________________
4. In this same scene, Kumail is acting like ____________________
5. Beth fell in love with Terry because ____________________
6. It seems like Beth and Terry found true love because ____________________
7. All the things Kumail's mother says to him in scene 4 are supposed ____________________
8. I think it is unfair of Kumail's parents to ____________________
9. Kumail's main criticism of his parents is that ____________________
10. Azmat says the American Dream means ____________________

3 Focus on analysis → SB, pp. 146–148

Find examples of humour in the text that match the context given here. Give line numbers.

Context	Example
1. Showing irritation that Kumail thinks he knows more than his brother.	
2. Naveed exaggerating to show that Kumail's confession isn't really that shocking.	
3. Naveed exaggerating the situation about their mother's feelings.	
4. Emily using humour to show irritation about the headshots.	

D Invisible identity?

1 Focus on analysis → SB, pp.150–152

a Fill in the table with information from the text. Give line numbers.

Problem	Solution
1. feeling depressed (l.16)	
2.	sick note with "stress" as reason (l.28)
3.	shared with line manager (ll.53–54)
4. acute psychosis (l.70)	
5.	met with line manager for lunch (ll.82–83)
6. returning to work (ll.84–85)	
7.	open up, speak up (l.107, ll.109–110)
8. not knowing how to react (ll.111–113)	

b Complete this analysis of the text's structure and its effects on the reader with the words and phrases.

clear overview | development | approach | hopeful | journey | optimistic outlook | solution-oriented | timeline | well-structured | inside views

Overall, I thought the text was ______________ 1 because it provided a ______________ 2 of the problems. Jamil doesn't just dwell on the problems but instead has a ______________ 3 perspective. The text was almost like a ______________ 4 as it led the reader from the narrator's time at college until his time as an employee. In this way, it was easy to see his ______________ 5 from uncertain and ill to confident and able to cope with his illness. His ______________ 6 to this difficult subject was very open and honest as he gives the readers ______________ 7 of his ______________ 8 without hiding anything. He seems to have an ______________ 9 in general and this also makes the reader feel ______________ 10.

2 Discussing mental health → SB, p.153

To help you prepare your discussion, match the following phrases to the groups of people in society and put them in the word web. Some phrases may match more than one group.

to fight misconceptions | to give unbureaucratic help | to offer in-house counselling | to offer paid sick leave | to promote mental health awareness | to take mental health seriously

Mental health issues

media
____
____
____
____

employers
____
____
____

mental health organisations
____
____
____
____
____

1 Lesen und Schreiben → SB, pp. 157–158

1 Words matter

Match the words from the text to the synonyms or explanations by looking at the context.

1. predominantly (l. 4)
2. diaspora (l. 7)
3. ingrained (l. 15)
4. to oscillate (l. 30)
5. to denote (l. 32)
6. cohort (l. 36)
7. ambiguity (l. 37)
8. phenotypical (l. 42)
9. blatantly (l. 75)
10. denigrating (l. 79)

A outward, physical characteristics
B to stand for sth, to symbolise
C being unclear, vague
D insulting, putting sb down
E people living far from their ancestral home
F to move back and forth between two points
G behaving very directly in a negative way
H a group of people with sth in common
I mostly, primarily
J deeply rooted or fixed in sb or sth

1	2	3	4	5	6	7	8	9	10

2 Reading for detail

a Assign the following words to the taxi driver, the host family in Langa and the person in Bo Kaap and sort them into the table. You can use some of the words more than once.

accepting | biased | bold | genuine | heartfelt | honest | impolite | insecure | judgemental | narrow-minded | open | opinionated | prejudiced | presumptuous | pushy | stubborn | superficial | tolerant | warm

Taxi driver	Host family in Langa	Person in Bo Kaap

b Write two sentences about each person's attitude towards the author.

1. ______________________________

____

____

2. ______________________________

____

____

3. ______________________________

____

____

2 Hörverstehen → SB, p.159

1 Before you listen, match the phrases from the listening text to the German translations.

1. on the verge of rescue
2. bewildered / dumbfounded face
3. half-hearted stab
4. soothing whispers
5. panicked dash
6. dash of racism
7. to hail from
8. to write sb off
9. to glean on your own
10. to take credit for sth

A verblüffter Gesichtsausdruck
B Hauch von Rassismus
C panisches Wegflitzen
D kurz vor der Rettung
E jdn abschreiben
F selbst herausbekommen
G beruhigendes Geflüster
H die Lorbeeren für etw ernten
I stammen aus
J halbherziger Versuch

A27 **2** Listen to the first part of the narrative and put these subheadings in the correct order.

- ☐ Welcome turns to cruelty
- ☐ First lesson in gratefulness
- ☐ Ignorant racism
- ☐ Unrecognisable to myself
- ☐ A time of 'peace'

A28 **3** Listen to the second part of the narrative and take notes in the table on these three topics.

Gratefulness	Assimilation	Stereotypes and prejudices

Hörverstehen

1 Pre-listening

Before you listen, think of possible positive and negative consequences of keeping a secret from a close friend. Take notes in the table below.

Positive consequences ☺	Negative consequences ☹

A29 2 Listening for gist

Listen to the podcast in which a gay sportsperson talks about his experiences. Decide whether the following statements are true or false.

	Statement	True	False
1.	From a very early age, Matthew had dreamed about a career in show business.		
2.	Matthew stopped trampolining because he did not like the typical clothes he had to wear for it.		
3.	Due to his feminine appearance and behaviour, Matthew was an easy target for people to make fun of.		
4.	When Matthew started his diving training, he did not know for sure yet that he was gay.		
5.	Matthew avoided coming out because it did not really matter from a performance perspective.		
6.	Even though Matthew was very successful at diving, he did not feel comfortable in his training group.		
7.	Once he turned 18, Matthew ended his career in diving and went back to trampolining.		

A29 ◁)) **3 Listening for detail**

Listen again and answer the following questions in keywords.

1. Why did Matthew enjoy trampolining? Name two reasons.

___

2. Why did Matthew feel like he couldn't come out to the people he trained with?

___

3. What were the consequences of Matthew avoiding coming out? Name two.

___

4. According to Jack, what are the two options that gay athletes are faced with?

___

5. Why did Matthew leave the sport in the end?

___

6. What did Matthew focus on after he had stopped diving?

___

4 Post-listening

a Write a short email to Matthew in which you comment on the difficulties he describes in the podcast and how these might be changed.

From:	...
To:	...
Subject:	Interview in the LGBT Sport Podcast

___

___

___

___

___

___

___

___

___

b In your opinion, outline possible reasons behind the "othering" that Matthew mentions.

___

___

___

___

___

Issues of globalisation

1 Crossword puzzle: Globalisation vocabulary → SB, pp. 160–161

Complete the crossword puzzle.

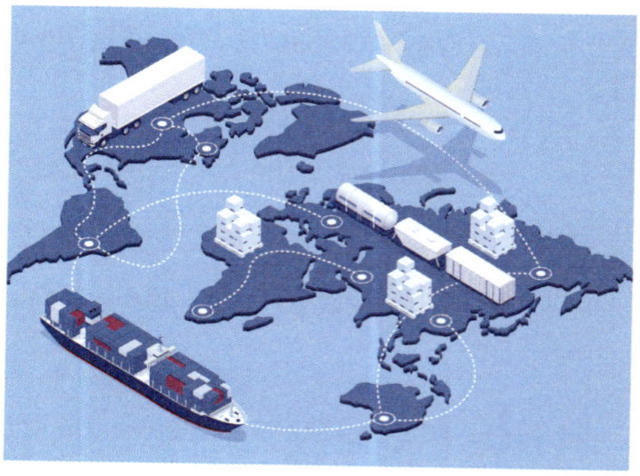

Across (→)

2. This is a key element of globalisation.
3. If three or more countries are involved in an agreement, it is called …
6. Another word for reducing the number of weapons.
7. The UN is an example of a global … spirit.
9. One effect of multinational companies is that they … the global economy.
12. Another word for moving or being moved freely and easily.
13. Another word for a large, often unfair difference.
14. Container ships play a big role in global …

Down (↓)

1. A … chain depends on the smooth process between production and distribution.
2. Protectionism uses … to further national interests.
3. Globalisation promotes the … of goods around the world.
4. In order for our planet to survive, we need global … of the important issues.
5. Poorer countries hope that globalisation will bring them …
8. Another word for an agreement between two or more governments.
10. The UN currently has 193 … states.
11. There are no … controls between countries that belong to the EU.

A Global work

1 Reading for detail → SB, pp.162–164

Find five things that made Arjun feel uncomfortable. Write a short description using your own words and give line numbers.

1. ______
2. ______
3. ______
4. ______
5. ______

2 Focus on analysis → SB, pp.162–164

a Read the section again about the young woman who has also come for an interview (ll. 21–30). Fill in the table with information about her appearance and verbs to describe her personality.

The young woman's appearance	Verbs describing her personality

b Use the following words and phrases to write at least 120 words comparing Arjun and the young woman.

awkward | Compared to Arjun, she ... | graceful | self-assured | self-centred | self-conscious | straightforward | tense | They couldn't be more unlike each other because ... | Compared to Arjun, she ... | The two characters differ in that ... | Whereas the young woman ..., Arjun ...

A30 3 Listening: Forward Thinking: Outsourcing → SB, p.164

Listen to the podcast and complete the following tasks.

1. Where does the guest, Steve Prescott, work?

____

____

2. Complete the sentence.

"Outsourcing basically means to arrange for somebody outside a company or an organisation to ____

____

____

3. If the third party company is situated in a country far away, then this is known as …

a ☐ longshoring. b ☐ offshoring. c ☐ outposting.

4. According to Steve Prescott, what simple guideline is there for deciding whether a company should outsource a business activity?

____

____

5. Which reason is given for the increased significance of outsourcing for the service sector in the 1990s?

____

____

6. Which are the leading outsourcing countries? Name at least three.

____

7. Steve Prescott is talking about some of the positives of outsourcing. Fill in the gaps.

"Outsourcing creates foreign investment which ____________________ economic growth and can lead to improvements in infrastructure and ____________________ in the economy. Moreover, it creates ____________________. Outsourcing has provided a new area of employment, especially for ____________________ with good standards of English and skills."

8. Which issues concerning working conditions and wages in factories in Bangladesh are mentioned? Name at least four.

____

____

____

____

____

____

Writing a blog post

→ SB, pp.165–166

1 Which of the following words describe Allison? Write line numbers next to the words that fit.

1. courageous	______	7. optimistic	______
2. depressed	______	8. positive	______
3. diligent	______	9. receptive	______
4. hard-working	______	10. relaxed	______
5. honest	______	11. strong-minded	______
6. independent	______	12. worrisome	______

2 **Writing Allison's blog post**

a Decide which topic these phrases could fit and sort them into the table below.

am I a bother? | asked us questions | can teach me | challenging work | company presentation | hard to remember their names | interesting tasks | interns with CEO | knew most info | like interview | met lots of people | nice but reserved | name tags | not feel welcome | not spill coffee | relaxed atmosphere | responsible for South American customers | took notes | showed interest in each of us | some new info | stressful morning | too many questions? | tough boss | very friendly

The new boss	
Meeting with CEO	
Colleagues	
Company tour	

b Decide on the order of the paragraphs for the blog post.

Paragraph 1: ______

Paragraph 2: ______

Paragraph 3: ______

Paragraph 4: ______

c Create an exclamation, rhetorical question or exaggeration to start the blog post.

______

d Use the words and phrases from this exercise, the photos and your own ideas to write Allison's blog post after her first day. Add sentences and connectors where necessary.

INTERNET

<1> Home <2> About <3> Blog <4> Info

B Working across cultures

1 Reading for gist → SB, pp.167–168

Give line numbers for the sections of the text that provide answers to these questions.

1. What are some benefits of working across different countries? ____________
2. What is a good way to handle your email inbox? ____________
3. What is a common problem with virtual meetings and how can you deal with it? ____________
4. What does patience have to do with communication? ____________
5. How can you deal with different accents? ____________
6. What can people gain from working across countries? ____________

2 Focus on analysis → SB, pp.167–169

a Read the scenario and underline keywords that illustrate the cross-cultural problems.

A German businessman has moved to Chicago to work for an American company. After a presentation to the department head, the German is talking to an American colleague about the presentation.

German: I showed my presentation to the department head, and she said it was okay.

American: Aren't you going to change anything?

German: No, I'm done with the presentation now.

American: But maybe there are some things you could improve.

German: Why?

American: Because she said it was okay but not good.

German: But when did she say it wasn't good?

American: She said it was only okay. Did you listen to how she said it?

b Note down the parts of the advice given in the text which apply best to this scenario.

____

c Analyse the scenario. Give a recommendation about who could have done what differently.

____

____

____

____

____

____

____

C Global trade

1 Reading for gist → SB, pp. 171–172

Skim the article and put these pieces of information in the correct order.

_____ Standardised containers led to larger ships.
_____ Almost all trade goods are transported by ship.
_____ Standardised containers helped to reduce costs.
_____ Different sized containers made trade more difficult.
_____ Standardised containers made globalisation possible.
_____ The banana in your kitchen arrived on a container ship.
_____ Containers have been used in international trade for centuries.
_____ The trend of transporting goods by ship is unlikely to slow down.
_____ An American businessman had the idea to standardise containers.
_____ The standardised shipping container plays a crucial role in the global supply chain.

2 Words matter → SB, pp. 171–173

Find words and phrases in the article that match the pictures below.

____

____

____

____

____

____

____

____

____

3 Focus on analysis → SB, pp. 171–173

Find quotes from the article matching the following arguments that highlight the positive or negative sides of globalisation. Give line numbers.

Argument	Quote
1. almost everything we own arrived from another country	
2. we all heavily rely on global trade	
3. early trade involved hard work, lots of time and was expensive	
4. globalisation has advanced our world	
5. global trade by sea has increased dramatically	
6. bigger is not always better	
7. the importance of trade by sea is often underestimated	

4 Listening: Forward Thinking: Transportation in the age of globalisation

a Before you listen, find a synonym to replace the underlined word.

1. The canal is vital to global trade. ______
2. Cars are made of hundreds of different components. ______
3. The repercussions of the accident were felt around the world. ______
4. The earth trembled for minutes during the earthquake. ______
5. How many cars can be assembled in one day in the factory? ______

A31 **b** Listen to the podcast. Match the numbers to the correct information or event.

1. 193 kilometres
2. 19,000
3. $89 million
4. 100,000
5. 90 %
6. 130,000
7. $4570
8. $230 billion

A number of cows stuck on ships in the Suez Canal
B value of goods on the Ever Given
C possible loss in global growth
D number of ships that go through the canal per year
E new, increased cost of shipping a container
F amount of uninsured cargo on stuck ships
G length of the Suez Canal
H number of unfinished Volkswagen cars in 2020

A31 **c** Listen to the podcast again and answer the questions in keywords.

1. What does the economist compare the global economy to? ______
2. What are the Suez Canal's advantages? ______
3. What are the repercussions of the logjam for consumers? ______

D Global economy?

1 Working with a diagram → SB, p. 175

Complete the explanation of the law of supply and demand using the following words.

availabilty | connected | decreases | demand | economic | factors | imbalance | increase | interact | lower | prices | quantity | results | shortage | supply | surplus | want | willingness

The law of supply and demand is an ______________ 1 principle that describes how sellers and buyers of a product ______________ 2 with each other. It also explains how the price of a product is ______________ 3 to whether people want to buy or sell it. In a simplified way, you can say that when prices ______________ 4, companies also raise the supply to make more money. But when there is more supply than demand, they ______________ 5 the prices so people will buy again. The same is true when prices go down: ______________ 6 also goes down, but later prices go back up. Supply describes the ______________ 7 of a product available, and demand means the ______________ 8 to buy and how much is wanted. In other words, this economic theory is "______________ 9 versus ______________ 10" and there is often an ______________ 11 between the two. Demand depends on ______________ 12 like the season, weather, holidays or popularity.

For example, if it is a rainy autumn, the ______________ 13 for umbrellas goes up. This higher demand leads to a ______________ 14 of umbrellas, which ______________ 15 in higher prices. Or if it is a warm winter, the demand for warm jackets ______________ 16. This means there is a ______________ 17 of jackets and the ______________ 18 decrease.

2 Reading for gist → SB, pp. 175–176

Divide the text into sections according to these five subheadings. Write line numbers for each section.

1. Applying the doughnut model to communities ______________
2. Describing the doughnut model ______________
3. Creating sweet visions ______________
4. The doughnut model in California ______________
5. Old versus new ______________

3 Reading for detail → SB, pp.175–177

Decide if these words and phrases refer to the doughnut model or the supply and demand curve as described by Raworth in the article and sort them into the boxes.

ecological ceiling | destroying the environment | extreme inequalities | fulfil basic needs | GDP increase | having what we need within our means | holistic approach | line keeps going up | living in excess | never-ending economic growth | not exhaust resources | preserving Earth | poverty | social foundation | universal method | within limits set by our planet

DOUGHNUT MODEL	SUPPLY AND DEMAND CURVE

4 Focus on analysis → SB, pp.175–177

Match the sentences to the five possible intentions of the text.

to argue

to describe

to inform

to instruct

to persuade

1. Our prices show a wave pattern, first up and then down. ______________
2. Listen, this new proposal is of great importance and you're wrong. ______________
3. This article will bring you up-to-date on our findings. ______________
4. Follow the example given below. ______________
5. If you look at it from my point of view, you will see the significance. ______________
6. I'm here to give you more details on the current situation. ______________
7. By repeating the process, you will achieve the following results. ______________
8. Your claims completely miss the point. ______________
9. The author portrays globalisation as a race car, fast and furious. ______________
10. I'm convinced the statistics will bring you around to our way of thinking. ______________
11. Let me explain the basics of the doughnut economic model to you. ______________
12. Try our method and I'm sure you'll like what you see. ______________

1 Lesen und Schreiben → SB, pp. 182–183

1 Reading for detail

Complete the sentences with information from the text, using your own words.

1. As logistics coordinator, Verena Mohaupt had to ______________________________
____
2. Safety precautions on the ship included ______________________________
____
3. Knitting was important to Verena because ______________________________
4. A big advantage of planning ahead is ______________________________
5. In addition to planning, it is important ______________________________
6. The expedition was almost cancelled because ______________________________

2 Writing an email

Imagine you are Verena aboard the Polarstern. Write an email to your friends and family about life on the ship. Use the following words, information from the article and your own ideas.

adventure | challenges | comfort | crew | freezing water | equipment | knitting supplies | logistics | no accidents | polar bears | pomegranates | safety precautions | solve problems

From:	…
To:	…
Subject:	

____

2 Hörverstehen → SB, p.184

A32 1 Listen to the first track and answer the questions in keywords.

1. What does Zoe say about being flexible?

___

___

2. What was the biggest disadvantage of using the mummy chair?

___

___

3. How does Zoe describe the food situation?

___

A33 2 Before you listen, fill in the correct English translation of these words from the second track. Then listen and check your answers.

1. The situation wasn't hopeless, but it was a big ___. (*Herausforderung*)
2. The first step to solving a problem is ___. (*Fehlersuche*)
3. Before the ship leaves, the ___ has to be stored in the hull. (*Schiffsladung*)
4. Moving the instruments onto the ice floe was ___. (*knifflig*)
5. The crew had to ___ the instruments from the water. (*bergen*)
6. If we ___ everything, it'll be easier to find later. (*beschriften*)
7. Luckily we didn't have to ___ any polar bears. (*umgehen mit*)
8. Don't worry if it breaks – we have a ___ that we can use. (*Ersatz*)

3 Kommunikation → SB, p.185

1 Sort the following words and phrases about the effects of globalisation into the table. If you are not sure, put the word or phrase in the midldle column. Add more words and phrases to each column.

capitalism | cheap labour | collaboration | competition | consumerism | exploitation | inequality | interdependency | integration | job insecurity | job opportunities | migration | mistrust | partnership | pollution | profit | self-sufficiency | solidarity | specialisation | understanding

Positive effects ☺	Could go either way 😐	Negative effects ☹

The world of work

1 Talking about the changing world of work

a Write down a caption and description for each picture. Use the words and phrases below to help you.

drone | shopping habits | robots | traditional jobs | personal contact | replacing human beings | consumption | postman | social interaction | parcel | occupation | exchange | skyline

A

B

b Compare picture A and picture B and describe the change.

A Why do we work?

1 Focus on grammar

a Use the ideas from the boxes to write conditional sentences types 1 and 2 about work-sharing and an unconditional basic income.

CONDITION

It becomes normal that two people share one job.

Job-sharing becomes the norm.

Everybody receives a certain amount of money, irrespective of their wealth or income.

An unconditional basic income is introduced.

Everyone has just enough money to get by.

CONSEQUENCE

… unemployment is reduced drastically.

… both parents in a family can pursue their careers.

… people have more time for their families and their hobbies.

… there are fewer stress-related illnesses.

… there is no one to do unpopular jobs.

… people are much happier because they can choose if they want to work or live a modest life.

… no one works any more.

… people still work because the income paid by the state is too little.

… the state is bankrupt within months.

____

____

____

____

____

____

____

b What would have happened if Keynes' predictions had come true? Form conditional sentences type 3.

… weekly working hours drop to about 15.
… people stop seeing the accumulation of money as an end in itself.
… industry stops producing more than is needed.
… people understand what it means to have enough.
… people learn to be content with living the good life.

If Keynes' predictions had come true, …

– ______________________________
– ______________________________
– ______________________________
– ______________________________
– ______________________________

2 Listening: Teleworking → SB, p. 190

a Before you listen, match these colloquial words and phrases from the listening text with their more formal definitions.

1. to drag on
2. a bit of a disaster
3. to stand out from the crowd
4. to get your head around sth
5. to be over the moon
6. to bounce ideas off sb
7. to keep up with sth

A to understand sth
B to do sth at an acceptable rate
C to be very pleased about sth
D a minor failure
E to go on for too long
F noticeably different from ordinary people or things
G to talk about sth with sb in an informal way in order to get an opinion

1	2	3	4	5	6	7

A34 **b** Listen to the six speakers and answer the following questions about them in keywords.

Speaker 1: What was he doing at home instead of sitting in traffic? Name two activities.

____

____

Speaker 2: Why is it hard for her to concentrate on work when she is in the office? Name two reasons.

____

____

Speaker 3: How does he try to keep his carbon footprint low? Name two aspects.

____

Speaker 4: Why does he struggle to work from home? Name two reasons.

____

Speaker 5: What does she miss about working in an office? Name three aspects.

____

____

Speaker 6: Why does she find it difficult to stand out from the crowd when working remotely?

____

B The future of money

1 Reading for detail → SB, pp.191–193

Read the short story excerpt and fill in the missing information.

1. The main character in the short story is called ____________. She lives in a flat in ______________.
2. In England, it is illegal to save ______________, but Roo still has __________________________ left to spend.
3. The system, by which everyone is paid the same wage, is called ______________________.
4. All people in England have access to free services like ______________________ ____.
5. If people don't want to work although they are fit and healthy, ______________________ or, if this does not work, ______________________________.
6. Roo does not have to lock her door, as there is no more ______________________.
7. It is the law that one-year-old products ______________________________ These places are there to ______________________________.
8. Roo's neighbour is called ______________ and is __________ years old. The neighbour sits down on top of ______________________________________. Her favourite topic is ______________________________ ____.
9. When the revolution took place, Roo was only ____________ years old.
10. Roo's father was called ______________. He was strongly against ______________________. He had a lot of ______________.
11. Roo's mother, on the other hand, was part of the ______________ which took place __________ years ago. She died during ______________________.
12. Roo is worried that she has inherited ________ ______________________________.
13. People who can't let go of their money are called ______________________.
14. Janice can't understand ______________ ______________________. She thinks that hoarding money is ______________.

2 Focus on analysis → SB, pp. 191–193

Decide whether the following excerpts indicate an inner or outer conflict that Roo is faced with. Explain why.

Excerpt	Conflict	Explanation
1. "There it was, in her hand. Ready to be spent. Ready to do what it was meant to do, be what it was meant to be. But she couldn't do it. She couldn't fight this urge any longer and she stuffed it back in her pocket and left the shop." (ll. 3–5)		
2. "She was going to save it. Hoard it. Gather it until she had piles hidden in her flat. Illegal, of course, and shameful. But Roo had made up her mind, this money, her money, was not being spent today." (ll. 5–7)		
3. "Deep down, she knew the state would find out. [...] The state analysts would [...] know that someone, somewhere, hadn't spent their full salary that month. [...] But they couldn't know it was her. Out of fifty-five million people in England, they couldn't know it was her." (ll. 12–25)		
4. "People were happy, Roo was happy. At least, she thought she was. But, sitting on her luxurious sofa, with all the latest technology and trinkets glimmering around her, she pulled out the unspent coins." (ll. 32–34)		
5. "Janice chuckled and then lowered herself onto Roo's sofa, right on top of the hoard. Roo winced, praying Janice wouldn't feel it through the cushion. For the first time, she wanted her neighbour out of the flat." (ll. 44–46)		
6. "Janice shuffled on the cushion and frowned. 'I think it's time you got a new sofa ...' Roo's eyes widened. 'Yes, it's coming up to one year. It's terribly uncomfortable and tatty now isn't it. Here, let me help you up.'" (ll. 72–75)		

Talking about likes and dislikes → SB, p.194

1 Read the dialogue between two friends talking about their workplaces and working conditions. Complete the text with the following verbs using gerund constructions.

be | catch up | have | involve | leave | look | ride | take care | wait | work

Milo: Hi, Lara. Nice to see you again.

Lara: Yes, you too. It's great to finally meet up again. I've missed ________________ 1 with each other.

Milo: That's right. And this is the first time I've seen you since you started your new job. So, tell me … How is it?

Lara: It's early days still, but so far so good. Our offices are in a modern high-rise building in the city centre. I get to work with the underground most of the time, but sometimes I go by bike. I prefer ________________ 2 my bike to work in the morning – it really wakes me up.

Milo: I bet! I think I know what building you mean. It's the one that looks like a cucumber, isn't it?

Lara: Yes, I suppose it does. I enjoy ________________ 3 in the city centre, but it's very noisy when the windows are open. I work in an open-plan office with about 25 other people. I don't really mind ________________ 4 with so many people but it can be quite hectic at times.

Milo: And what are your colleagues like?

Lara: Fine. There's a great atmosphere in the office. I work in a team of six people and we all get on really well together.

Milo: That's great. And what exactly is it that you do? I know it's something to do with marketing.

Lara: Yes, I work in the marketing department. My job involves ________________ 5 of international customers and their marketing campaigns. There's always plenty to do!

Milo: I can imagine … What are the working hours like?

Lara: The hours are one of the best things about the job. I work flexitime with core hours. I love ________________ 6 work early in the morning. It's when I feel the most creative.

Milo: Lucky you! My job is a nine-to-five job with a half-hour lunch break. There's no flexibility at all. It's quite frustrating. And we're expected to work unpaid overtime when necessary. You know, I actually feel like ________________ 7 my job.

Lara: Yes, it was like that in my last job. In fact, it was the lack of flexibility that made me want to leave, along with the pay. In my new company, lots of employees are trade union members. ________________ 8 better working conditions is the result of a recent labour agreement.

Milo: And how is your pay now?

Lara: Great! I have a take-home pay of about £2,500 a month. Plus, we get a Christmas bonus!

Milo: Wow! I think I'd better start ________________ 9 for a new job! There's no point in ________________ 10 any longer.

C Inequality at work

1 Reading for gist → SB, pp.195–196

Read the text and choose a suitable heading and a function for each paragraph.

Paragraph	Heading	Function
1		
2		
3		
4		
5		
6		

A Still a long road ahead
B How to tackle the problem
C Inequality from the beginning
D Study reveals scope of inequality
E The problem goes beyond gender
F Young ethnic minorities groups worried

a Short introduction of topic and outline of issue
b Account of actions that should be taken to tackle gender pay gap
c Summary of survey results on students' worries regarding final grades
d Depiction of detailed study results on gender pay gap to illustrate problem
e Shift of focus from gender pay gap to career prospects related to ethnic background
f Account of concerns related to career prospects of BAME students as well as women

2 Listening: More or Less: Gender pay gap → SB, p.198

a Before you listen, choose the correct synonym for these words taken from the podcast. Use a dictionary to help you.

1. claim — a ☐ definition — b ☐ statement — c ☐ dispute
2. to distinguish — a ☐ to combine — b ☐ to separate — c ☐ to compare
3. entitlement — a ☐ right — b ☐ regulation — c ☐ result
4. mean — a ☐ temporary — b ☐ minimum — c ☐ average
5. cohort — a ☐ group — b ☐ collection — c ☐ association

A35 **b** Listen and complete the sentences with information from the podcast.

1. According to the Institute of Fiscal Studies (IFS) the gender pay gap between men and women widens steadily after ______________________
2. There are no statistics on unequal pay because ______________________
3. If you wanted to make the gender pay gap appear really big, you would have to include ______________________
4. Just looking at female workers, part-timers earn ______________________
5. In contrast to the IFS, Fraser Nelson compared the earnings of ______________________
6. The IFS, which includes part-timers, finds that even for younger cohorts, ______________________

D Workforce of the future

1 Reading for detail → SB, pp. 199–200

Look at the key points from the article and complete the table with detailed information from the text.

Key points	Information from the text
1. Japan is changing	
2. The security guard Ugo	
3. Japan's attitude towards robots	
4. Robots in Tokyo's Silver Wing nursing home	
5. The West's attitude towards robots	

2 Focus on grammar

Use the following words to make a positive statement (+), a negative statement (–) or a question (?) using the will-future.

1. robots / replace / pets / in the year 2090 (?)

____

2. artificial intelligence / be able / interact / emotionally / with humans (–)

____

____

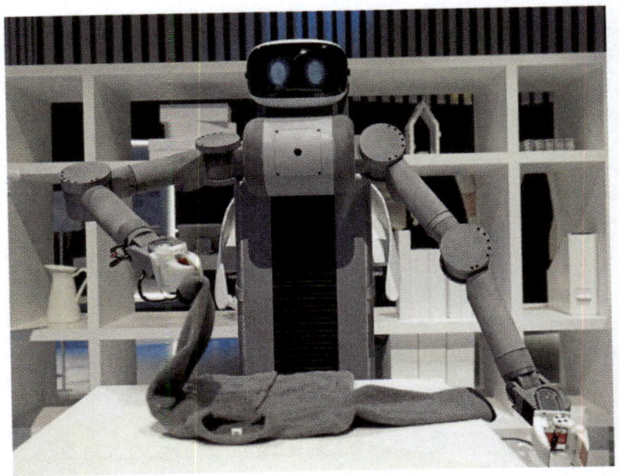

3. artificial intelligence / start / a revolution / against mankind (?)

____

4. humans / depend / on humanoid robots / in various jobs (+)

____

5. mankind / stop / developing artificial intelligence / improve / living conditions (–)

____

A36 3 Listening: Forward Thinking: Diversity in the workplace

a Listen to the podcast and decide which sentence sums up its message correctly.

- ☐ Diversity in the workplace is a challenge, especially for women.
- ☐ Diversity is a fact in British society and it must be dealt with in a constructive way.
- ☐ Diversity is widely discussed in the US as a solution for more productivity in the economy.

b Choose the correct sentence parts to summarise the information given on each of these issues.

1 Diversity in the workplace

2 Homogenous teams

3 Advantages of diverse teams

4 Disadvantages of diversity in the workplace

5 Diversity is reality:

A are a contributing factor to the growth of companies.

B people with autism are an enrichment in such a team because they can see things from a different angle.

C refers to issues of gender, race, age, disabilities and even educational background.

D can create communication problems when people are not open enough to overcome their cultural perceptions.

E the unequal payment which comes with diversity.

F make it easier for employers to communicate with employees and find compromises more quickly.

G the management has full responsibility for the hiring policy.

H we have to find strategies to cope with the challenges diverse teams bring and unlock the potential.

1	2	3	4	5

c Listen to the podcast again and answer the following questions in keywords.

1. According to Dr Martin, why can diverse teams be more productive than homogenous ones? Name two reasons.

____

____

2. Why may diverse teams slow down projects and work processes?

____

3. Which rules does Dr Martin suggest everybody follows to avoid problems caused by cultural concepts and diverse ethnic backgrounds?

____

1 Lesen und Schreiben → SB, pp. 206–207

1 Reading for detail

Read the text and complete the following tasks.

1. Name three factors that James Neely mentions which help him feel comfortable at work.

____

____

2. Write down two positive characteristics often found in people with autism as mentioned in the text.

____

3. Note down three problems each which dyspraxia can cause …
   - neurologically: ______________________________
   - in the workplace: ______________________________
4. Name two advantages that dyspraxic people can contribute at work.

____

2 Focus on analysis

Match each paragraph of the text with its function.

ll. 1–4	A example case study
ll. 5–17	B suggestions for the future
ll. 18–34	C development of case study
ll. 35–45	D headline and introduction of the topic
ll. 46–81	E arguments for, with real-life examples
ll. 82–102	F statistical information, why the topic is relevant

3 Writing an argumentative essay

a Take notes on opportunities and challenges of working in a diverse team in the table.

Opportunities	Challenges

b Would you like to work in a diverse team? Write four sentences and give reasons.

____

____

____

____

4 Writing a speech

Complete the manuscirpt of a speech with the following words. There are two words you do not need.

acceptance | angle | attention | challenges | departments | disadvantages | employees | forward | future | hiring | image | immensely | impairments | neurological | opportunity | overcome | varied | workforce

Dear colleagues,

I would like to use this ______ 1 to talk about an important issue, and one which I think could take our company ______ 2. I would like to talk about disabilities. During my internship, I've had the chance to work in many different ______ 3 and I've noticed that we have very few ______ 4 with disabilities. This raises the question why this is the case.

Firstly, it's important to point out that the term 'disability' is ______ 5 and does not simply refer to someone who experiences physical ______ 6. There are many forms of disability and we should be aware of these and open to understanding and ______ 7.

I believe that by ______ 8 more employees with disabilities, regardless of whether physical, ______ 9 or otherwise, our company could benefit ______ 10. For example, people with disabilities can often be more creative, pay more ______ 11 to detail, and generally look at problems from another ______ 12. Furthermore, a more diverse ______ 13 would have a positive effect on the team and could give the company a more positive ______ 14.

I am aware that there are ______ 15 connected to employing people with disabilities, but I think that this company has the potential to ______ 16 these and grow with them.

2 Hörverstehen → SB, p. 207

1 Before you listen, guess the German translations for these words and phrases from the podcast. Use a bilingual dictionary to check your answers.

English	German translation
1. eligible	
2. parental leave	
3. financial setback	
4. chicken pox	
5. exacerbated	
6. ingrained	

A37 2 Listen and complete the sentences with information from the podcast.

1. According to analysis by the University of Birmingham, only 1% of eligible parents in the UK took advantage of ______________________________

____
2. Fathers that take extended time off to look after their kids often feel ______________________________
3. When Ian Blithe's first child was six months old, he decided ______________________________
4. Ian found it very difficult to get the self-confidence to ______________________________
5. He had to leave a photo shoot in the forest because ______________________________

____
6. Ian noticed the misconceptions of people in his village regarding male childcare, especially when he

____

3 Kommunikation

→ SB, pp. 208–209

1 Collect positive and negative effects on the world of work regarding the developments listed in the table below.

	Positive effects ☺	Negative effects ☹
1. Teleworking		
2. Automation		
3. AI		
4. Diverse society		

Hörverstehen

1 Pre-listening

Before you listen, take notes on the aspects listed in the table below regarding our relationship with work. You may use the internet or other resources to help you.

Reasons why we work	
How our relationship with work has evolved over time	
Possible changes in the future	

A38 2 Listening for gist

Listen to the podcast on changes in the world of work. Choose the correct answer from the options (a, b or c) given below. There is only one correct answer.

1. Loss of jobs leads to …
   - a ☐ an increased sense of self-worth.
   - b ☐ a rise in mental health problems.
   - c ☐ a growth of industry in communities like Youngstown.
2. The main goal of hunter-gatherers was to …
   - a ☐ plant and grow food on farms.
   - b ☐ increase their population numbers.
   - c ☐ take care of their immediate survival needs.
3. After their tasks for the day were done, the Ju/'hoansi people would …
   - a ☐ hold large social gatherings.
   - b ☐ focus on meaningful thoughts.
   - c ☐ spend time on hobbies and social interaction.
4. In comparison to people in modern societies, the Ju/'hoansi have …
   - a ☐ fewer material things.
   - b ☐ a worse work-life balance.
   - c ☐ a high motivation to work more efficiently.
5. Modern societies produce …
   - a ☐ just enough things to satisfy our needs.
   - b ☐ far too many things that we actually do not need.
   - c ☐ things that are sold and consumed all over the world.

A38 3 Listening for detail

Listen again and answer the following questions in keywords.

1. What are possible consequences for workers if an industry begins to decline? Name three.
2. Which historical development led to our current attitude towards work?
3. How were work and idleness viewed in farming societies?
4. How much time did the Ju/'hoansi people spend looking for food each week?
5. According to classical economists, why do we work?
6. What can we infer to be a major misconception about how our hunter-gatherer ancestors organised their society?

4 Post-listening

a James mentions that the Ju/'hoansi spend much of their time doing things which do not count as 'work'. Note down benefits and drawbacks of a hunter-gatherer lifestyle in the table below.

Benefits	Drawbacks

b Using your own ideas and the following words and phrases, explain how you think the world of work will change over the coming years.

remote working | work-life balance | equal pay | communication technology | brain drain | globalisation | unemployment | material wealth | equal opportunity

Trackliste

Topic / Extra Listening	Track	Spieldauer
Topic 1	Track 1: Forward Thinking: Eco-cities	07:57
	Track 2: Forward Thinking: The UN's Sustainable Development Goals	09:10
	Track 3: Green technology and early adoption – Part 1	03:34
	Track 4: Green technology and early adoption – Part 2	04:32
Topic 2	Track 5: Forward Thinking: Project Africa Digital	08:18
	Track 6: Report about GMOs	05:22
	Track 7: Robots on the road – Part 1	01:30
	Track 8: Robots on the road – Part 2	03:29
	Track 9: Robots on the road – Part 3	03:53
Extra listening 1	Track 10: Census goes digital in India	04:42
Topic 3	Track 11: Different ways of shopping	05:14
	Track 12: Forward Thinking: Marketing your business – Part 1	03:55
	Track 13: Forward Thinking: Marketing your business – Part 2	03:45
	Track 14: Smart Consumer: Second-hand clothes	05:03
	Track 15: Money matters	04:51
Topic 4	Track 16: Forward Thinking: The USA – past and present	07:06
	Track 17: Forward Thinking: DREAMers	06:18
	Track 18: The space race	04:31
	Track 19: Does America have its own civil religion?	11:48
Extra listening 2	Track 20: Life in the USA	06:27
	Track 21: There are as many identities in Northern Ireland as people	04:22
Topic 5	Track 22: A United Kingdom	04:31
	Track 23: Legacies of British slave ownership	06:17
	Track 24: Loose Ends – Part 1	04:59
	Track 25: Loose Ends – Part 2	04:55
Topic 6	Track 26: Forward Thinking: Diversity in society	09:24
	Track 27: The ungrateful refugee: 'We have no debt to repay' – Part 1	04:50
	Track 28: The ungrateful refugee: 'We have no debt to repay' – Part 2	05:34
Extra listening 3	Track 29: LGBT Sport Podcast	04:56
Topic 7	Track 30: Forward Thinking: Outsourcing	06:59
	Track 31: Forward Thinking: Transportation in the age of globalisation	09:03
	Track 32: The Ice Pod – Part 1	05:47
	Track 33: The Ice Pod – Part 2	06:06
Topic 8	Track 34: Teleworking	03:51
	Track 35: More or Less: Gender pay gap	03:51
	Track 36: Forward Thinking: Diversity in the workplace	07:47
	Track 37: Changing World of Work	03:15
Extra listening 4	Track 38: Automation Nation: Are we heading for a world without work?	05:00

Quellennachweis

4 CartoonStock Ltd, Bath (Greenberg, Steve); **5.1** ShutterStock.com RF, New York (f11photo); **5.2** ShutterStock.com RF, New York (MEzairi); **5.3** ShutterStock.com RF, New York (Bucchi Francesco); **6** https://creativecommons.org/licenses/by-sa/4.0/deed.de, Mountain View ; CC-BY-SA-4.0 Lizenzbestimmungen: https://creativecommons.org/licenses/by-sa/4.0/legalcode, https://www.statista.com/chart/19127/biggest-producers-of-beef/ Quelle: FAO, U.S. Department of Agriculture, siehe *3; **8** United Nations Sustainable Development Goals: https://www.un.org/sustainabledevelopment/ The content of this publication has not been approved by the United Nations and does not reflect the views of the United Nations or its officials or Member States; **9** ShutterStock.com RF, New York (Merkushev Vasiliy); **10.1** ShutterStock.com RF, New York (kichikimi); **10.2** ShutterStock.com RF, New York (AleksOrel); **10.3** ShutterStock.com RF, New York (AleksOrel); **10.4** ShutterStock.com RF, New York (AleksOrel); **10.5** ShutterStock.com RF, New York (AmySachar); **10.6** ShutterStock.com RF, New York (AleksOrel); **11** ShutterStock.com RF, New York (Juice Flair); **12** Getty Images Plus, München (E+ / simonkr); **14** Getty Images Plus, München (iStock Editorial / leighcol); **16.1** CartoonStock Ltd, Bath (Steve Greenberg); **16.2** CartoonStock Ltd, Bath (Chris Madden); **17** ShutterStock.com RF, New York (xfilephotos); **18.1** Getty Images Plus, München (iStock / alexsl); **18.2** ShutterStock.com RF, New York (Jevanto Productions); **18.3** Getty Images Plus, München (iStock / shapecharge); **18.4** stock.adobe.com, Dublin (Syda Productions); **19** ShutterStock.com RF, New York (Riccardo Mayer); **20** Getty Images Plus, München (E+ / Bartosz Hadyniak); **21** stock.adobe.com, Dublin (Artur); **23** Getty Images, München (Getty Images Entertainment / Slaven Vlasic); **24.1** IMAGO, Berlin (Image Source); **24.2** ShutterStock.com RF, New York (suicidecrew); **24.3** Ernst Klett Verlag GmbH, Stuttgart; **24.4** ShutterStock.com RF, New York (suicidecrew); **25** iStockphoto, Calgary, Alberta (Jamie Farrant); **27.1** ShutterStock.com RF, New York (Artishok); **27.2** ShutterStock.com RF, New York (r2dpr); **27.3** Getty Images Plus, München (iStock Unreleased / JasonDoiy); **28** ShutterStock.com RF, New York (indigo_design); **29** Pflügner, Matthias, Berlin; **30.1** ShutterStock.com RF, New York (Lucky Business); **30.2** ShutterStock.com RF, New York (Natalia Deriabina); **30.3** ShutterStock.com RF, New York (Tirachard Kumtanom); **30.4** ShutterStock.com RF, New York (Pixel-Shot); **32** stock.adobe.com, Dublin (tandav); **33.1** ShutterStock.com RF, New York (Prostock-studio); **33.2** Pflügner, Matthias, Berlin; **34.1** ShutterStock.com RF, New York (Josep Suria); **34.2** ShutterStock.com RF, New York (G-Stock Studio); **35** stock.adobe.com, Dublin (tujuh17belas); **36.1** ShutterStock.com RF, New York (ayzek); **36.2** ShutterStock.com RF, New York (DSBfoto); **36.3** Getty Images Plus, München (iStock / bonetta); **36.4** Getty Images Plus, München (Photodisc / Jeffrey Hamilton); **37** Bláha, Marek, Offenbach am Main; **38** ShutterStock.com RF, New York (shop_py); **39** stock.adobe.com, Dublin (Daylight Photo); **42** Getty Images Plus, München (iStock / rarrarorro); **43** ShutterStock.com RF, New York (EQRoy); **44** Alamy stock photo, Abingdon (TCD/Prod.DB); **45** akg-images, Berlin (Glasshouse/ Circa Images); **47** ShutterStock.com RF, New York (Sheila Fitzgerald); **49.1** NASA, Washington , D.C.; **49.2** Ernst Klett Verlag GmbH, Stuttgart; **49.3** Ernst Klett Verlag GmbH, Stuttgart; **51.1** ddp media GmbH, Hamburg (abaca press); **51.2** Getty Images, München (Stock Montage/Stock Montage); **52.1** ShutterStock.com RF, New York (suicidecrew); **52.2** Ernst Klett Verlag GmbH, Stuttgart; **52.3** Alamy stock photo, Abingdon (Dom Slike); **54** CartoonStock Ltd, Bath (Ron McGeary); **55** Getty Images Plus, München (Stephen Barnes); **57** ShutterStock.com RF, New York; **60** Getty Images Plus, München (E+ / SolStock); **61** Schobel, Ingrid, Hannover ; Quelle: National Records of Scotland, 2018; (Projected population change, 2018 to 2028 in Scotland); **62** iStockphoto, Calgary, Alberta (Jamie Farrant); **63** Picture Press, Hamburg (Picture Press/ROTA); **64** ©2022, Independent Food Aid Network, www.foodaidnetwork.org.uk; **65.1** ShutterStock.com RF, New York (suicidecrew); **65.2** Ernst Klett Verlag GmbH, Stuttgart; **67** laif, Köln (Francesco Guidicini/CAMERA PRESS); **68.1** Getty Images, München (Stockbyte); **68.2** Getty Images Plus, München (E+ / MesquitaFMS); **68.3** Getty Images Plus, München (E+ / South_agency); **68.4** Getty Images, München (MITO images / Niedring/Drentwett); **73** CartoonStock Ltd, Bath (Fishman, Loren); **74** Pflügner, Matthias, Berlin; **75** Getty Images Plus, München (Moment Open / Dave Williams); **79** ddp media GmbH, Hamburg (Celine Nieszawer/opale.photo/lai); **81** ShutterStock.com RF, New York (lazyllama); **82** ShutterStock.com RF, New York (Golden Sikorka); **84.1** stock.adobe.com, Dublin (stankevskaya); **84.2** ShutterStock.com RF, New York (Pixparts); **86.1** ShutterStock.com RF, New York (fizkes); **86.2** ShutterStock.com RF, New York (fizkes); **87** Getty Images Plus, München (iStock / Peopleimages); **88.1** ShutterStock.com RF, New York (Adisa); **88.2** Getty Images Plus, München (iStock / adventtr); **88.3** stock.adobe.com, Dublin (Maksym Yemelyanov); **88.4** Getty Images Plus, München (E+ / guenterguni); **88.5** ShutterStock.com RF, New York (Sergio Bertino); **88.6** Getty Images Plus, München (iStock / cometary); **88.7** Getty Images Plus, München (iStock / Melissa Kopka); **88.8** ShutterStock.com RF, New York (passkphoto); **88.9** ShutterStock.com RF, New York (gkrphoto); **91.1** ShutterStock.com RF, New York (Vectorium); **91.2** ShutterStock.com RF, New York (Vectorium); **91.3** ShutterStock.com RF, New York (Vectorium); **91.4** ShutterStock.com RF, New York (Vectorium); **91.5** ShutterStock.com RF, New York (Vectorium); **93** VISUM Foto GmbH, München (Dr. Hans-Peter Marschall); **94.1** Getty Images Plus, München (E+ / vm); **94.2** Getty Images Plus, München (iStock / Shutter2U); **96** Getty Images Plus, München (iStock / RomoloTavani); **97** ShutterStock.com RF, New York (fizkes); **99** Getty Images Plus, München (E+ / bojanstory); **101** Picture-Alliance, Frankfurt/M. (REUTERS); **103.1** ShutterStock.com RF, New York (howcolour); **103.2** ShutterStock.com RF, New York (howcolour); **104.1** ShutterStock.com RF, New York (suicidecrew); **104.2** Ernst Klett Verlag GmbH, Stuttgart; **105** ShutterStock.com RF, New York (Anna Kraynova); **106** Alamy stock photo, Abingdon (Neil Harris); **107** Pflügner, Matthias, Berlin; **Umschlag** Getty Images RF, München (Hero Images)

*3 Lizenzbestimmungen zu CC-BY-SA-4.0 siehe: http://creativecommons.org/licenses/by-sa/4.0/legalcode

Notes

Notes

Notes